JN084366

Reading in More Action

Tetsuhito Shizuka

KINSEIDO

Kinseido Publishing Co., Ltd.

3-21 Kanda Jimbo-cho, Chiyoda-ku,
Tokyo 101-0051, Japan

First published 2024 by Kinseido Publishing Co., Ltd.

Cover design: Takayuki Minegishi
Text design:　DAITECH co., ltd.

🎧 音声ファイル無料ダウンロード

https://www.kinsei-do.co.jp/download/4197

この教科書で 🎧 DL 00 の表示がある箇所の音声は、上記 URL または QR コードにて
無料でダウンロードできます。自習用音声としてご活用ください。

- ▶ PC からのダウンロードをお勧めします。スマートフォンなどでダウンロードされる場合は、
  ダウンロード前に「解凍アプリ」をインストールしてください。
- ▶ URL は、**検索ボックスではなくアドレスバー (URL 表示欄)** に入力してください。
- ▶ お使いのネットワーク環境によっては、ダウンロードできない場合があります。

🔘 CD 00　左記の表示がある箇所の音声は、教室用 CD（Class Audio CD）に収録されています。

はしがき

　英語のリーディング授業の目的は何でしょうか。その文章の内容を理解すること？　もちろんそれは必要なことです。しかし**文章の内容自体の把握が目的ならば、同じ内容について最初から日本語で書いてある文章を読んだ方が早いでしょう**。それをあえて英語で読むのは、そのようなトレーニングをすることによって、後々に自力でそのような英語を理解する能力を養成するためです。

　このような一見当たり前に思えることをあえて確認したのは、**英語のリーディング授業の目的が英語力の養成であることを忘れ、その文章の内容の把握が到達目標であるかのような学習方法をとる人が意外に多いからです。**

　例えば、英文を読んで日本語に訳すことばかりをしているとどうなるでしょうか。英文和訳とは、英文を読んでその意味を考え、それを日本語で表現しなおすという営みです。いわば英語から出発して日本語に到達して終わる作業です。英文の意味を正確に把握するために日本語で表現してみることは確かに役立つ部分もあるのですが、英語力を伸ばす上では実は大きな落とし穴があります。それは、最後に到達するのが日本語であるため注意が日本語表現に集中してしまうことです。こうなると、**記憶に残るのは日本語で表現された内容ばかりで、肝心の英語表現はさっぱり覚えていない**、ということが起こりえます。

　高校時代に、英文和訳が出題されるテスト対策として、和訳自体を丸暗記していった人はいませんか。そのような作業は、そのテストで点が取れたとしても、英語力を伸ばすこととは無関係であることは言うまでもありません。**英語力を高めるためには、英文を読んだ後で、「内容」自体ではなく、「内容を表していた英語表現」が記憶に残るような学習をしなければならない**のです。

　本テキスト *Reading in More Action*は、リーディングにおける内容の把握を到達点ではなくむしろ出発点ととらえ、その内容を表現していた英語をさまざまなタスクの中でアウトプットすることで、**マテリアルで使われていた語彙や表現や英文を自分のものにする**ことを目標に編された *Reading in Action*（2009）、*Reading in Action Basic*（2016）の流れを受け継ぐ最新のリーディングテキストです。「倫理的消費」「インクルーシブ教育」「性的マイノリティ」「男性の育児休暇」など、**今日必ず知っておかなければならないホットなトピックについて読みながら、ペアワークやグループワークの形で、英語表現をたくさん聞き、また口にできるように構成**してあります。

　一つのユニットが終わった後には、（1）**そのマテリアルで使われていた主要な語彙、表現、英文がすらすらと口をついて出るようになり**、（2）**その英文内容を簡単な英語で要約できるようになり**、（3）**扱われていたテーマについて自分の意見がある程度言えて書けるようになる**、ことを目標としています。

　ご存じのように、英語が使えることの重要性は年々高まるばかりです。皆さんは本テキストを活用して、自分の将来を切り開くための本物の英語力を是非身に付けてください。

編著者

本テキストの効果的な使い方（学生の皆さんへ）

　本テキストは、英文の内容をまずは正確に読み取ることを出発点として、それに加えてそこに使われていた語句や英語表現などを自分のものとして身に付けること、それらを使って自分の意見を述べることを目標に作られています。皆さんには以下のような学習方法をお薦めします。

1st Reading

　まずは一度、本文を自力で通読（黙読）してみましょう。英文タイトルを読み、それに付されている日本語（英文タイトルの直訳ではなく、日本語として全体をまとめているキャッチコピー的なものです）を読んで内容を予測しながら、第1段落から最後の段落まで、意味を考えながら読んでみます。

　英文を読むのに慣れている度合いにもよりますが、意味の切れ目と思われる箇所にスラッシュ（／）を付けたり、表現のまとまりと思われる語句を四角かっこ（[　　　]）で囲んだり、挿入語句だと思われる箇所に丸かっこ（(　　)）を付けたりするのもお勧めです。

　分からない単語が出てきてもこの段階では我慢して辞書は引かず、意味を推測しながら最後まで読み切ってみましょう。多少分からない箇所があっても読み進む力（「曖昧さに対する耐性」"tolerance for ambiguity"）をつけることも大切だからです。

2nd Reading

　ダウンロード音声を1文ずつ再生して、単語の発音はもちろん、強く読まれる箇所（その文の新情報である可能性が高いです）、わずかにポーズが置かれる箇所（文法的、構文的な切れ目である可能性が高いです）を確認し、場合によってはそれらに適宜印を付けながら、今度は知らない単語は辞書で確認しながら読んでみましょう。

　辞書でその語の最初に挙げてある訳語に飛びつくのでなく、その文脈に合った品詞・訳語を吟味します。また可能なかぎり英英辞典（ネット上にも優れた辞書があります）も利用すると、さらに英語力がついていきます。次に述べる、**Chunking** と同時並行で行ってもよいでしょう。

Chunking

　本文中の英語のかたまり（chunk）の日本語訳を見ながら、それに相当する英語部分を探す活動です。ダウンロード音声には正解が録音されていますので、一つ一つ確認しながら進むとよいでしょう。

　日本語訳に対応する英語を確認するということは、裏返せば英語の日本語訳を確認することにもなりますので、**2nd Reading** のヒントにもなる活動です。目標は、日本語訳を聞くだけで対応する英語をすぐに言えるようになることです。指示に従ってペアワークで練習するとよいでしょう。

Choosing

　本文の最も大切な内容を5つの文にまとめたものを、選択肢によって完成させる活動です。**2nd Reading** と **Chunking** の後であれば、どちらが true であるかはすぐに分かるはずです。また、ダウンロード音声で確認もできます。true の選択肢が確認できたらそこで終わらず、そちらの選択肢を入れた文を、教科書を見ずに言う練習をしてください。この5つの文を続けて言えれば、本文の要約ができていることになります。これも指示に従ってペアワークをすると効果的です。

Oral Reading

　これは本文に関連する3つの文を、音声面に細心の注意を払って音声化（音読、さらには見ずに言ってみる read and look up）の練習をすることで、皆さんの英語をより英語らしいものにするための活動です。英語の強弱リズムやリンキング、呑み込まれるように発音される部分が可視化された英文を見ながらダウンロード音声を聞き、まずは英語音声のイメージを確認してください。次にそれを真似て音読してみます。

　この **Oral Reading** の3つの文もやはり続けて言えば本文全体のポイントが浮かび上がるように作ってありますから、できれば覚えてしまうまで練習すると効果的です。

Defining

　英語の定義を読んで、それに当たる語を探す活動です。ターゲット語を当てるのと同じかそれ以上に、その英語定義のほうを理解し、英語による定義の仕方を学ぶことが英語力アップに役立つ活動です。ペアワークの指示を一歩進めて、英語定義のほうを何も見ずに言ってみることにトライすることをお勧めします。もちろん一人で行うこともできます。

Repeating

　Defining の正解の語あるいはその変化形・派生語を用いた文を完成する活動です。例文はいずれも短めですから、ワーキングメモリに入れて（一瞬覚えて）一気に言ってみることが十分に可能になっています。ダウンロード音声で答えを確認して終わりにせず、是非そこまでやってみましょう。そのような積み重ねで少しずつ英語を話す地力がついていきます。

Retelling

　本文の内容のポイントを、自分なりに口頭で再生する（retell する）活動です。本文で使われたキーワードやフレーズが、箇条書きの番号や、関連性や因果関係などを表すシンプルな矢印などの記号とともに提示されています。

　まずは全体を眺めながら、内容を思い出してみましょう。思い出せない部分があれば、本文のそれらしい箇所を再読してみてください。内容が思い出せたなら、これらのキーワード（名詞、動詞、形容詞などの「内容語」が中心です）に、機能語（前置詞、冠詞、be 動詞、助動詞など文法的な機能を担う語）を補いながら、センテンスにして言ってみましょう。

この時、決して言うべきことを全て書き出してはいけません。キーワードのみを見ながら、頭のなかで機能語を補いながら話すことで、スピーキング力が鍛えられるからです。

　ダウンロード音声は単なる一例なので、あくまで参考にするにとどめ、自分なりの表現で話してみるのが大切です。最終的には1分間程で全部言えるようになることを目指してください。

Commenting

　総仕上げとして、本文で述べられている事柄や意見などについて、自分なりに英語でコメントする活動です。本テキストは、議論を呼んだり、異論を持つ人が必ずいたりするようなトピックを数多く扱っています。テキスト内容を受動的に理解しただけで終わらず、理解した内容について自分が感じたことや思ったことを是非英語で表現してみましょう。

　与えられた文のなかで自分の考えと近いものがあれば、そのまま「覚えて」言ってみるだけでもとりあえずの「意見表明」になります。自分の考えと反対のものがあれば、Some say ... に続けてその文を言い、最後に but I have a different idea. などと言って、自分の考えを説明してみましょう。いくつか組み合わせたり、さらに自分のオリジナルな意見を付け加えたりすればさらに内容が豊かになるでしょう。ペアになって考えを言い合い、相手の意見に対してさらに自分の意見が言えるようになることが大切です。

CONTENTS

本テキストの効果的な使い方（学生の皆さんへ）

Let Us Be Ethical Consumers

倫理的消費に取り組み始めたアパレル産業

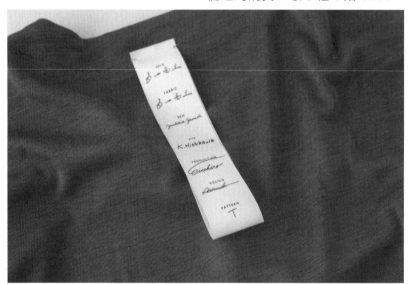

EQUALAND -TRUST AND INTIMATE- / Produced by ONEO Ltd.

Reading

CD1-02 ~ CD1-11

1 TOKYO—Apparel makers are increasingly creating products in ways that
2 take into consideration the human rights of those involved in production and
3 the environment. Such moves are aimed at raising brand value by tapping into
4 demand among people looking for such products in so-called ethical consumption.

5 Ethical consumption is expected to present opportunities for tackling issues
6 such as human rights violations and environmental destruction.

7 Equaland Trust and Intimate, a brand that uses natural materials, attaches
8 a "tag of trust" to its products. The tag, inscribed with the signatures of cotton
9 producers and designers, certifies that the brand is determined to reduce its
10 environmental impact and that it protects the human rights of its producers.

11 The 2013 collapse of a garment factory in Bangladesh triggered a global
12 movement in the apparel industry to review poor working conditions. Last year,
13 allegations of forced labor surfaced in China's Xinjiang region. Equaland's tag is a
14 reflection of its commitment to tackling such dark legacies of the apparel industry.

15 "Those who make clothes have been oppressed and not been able to express
16 their anger," said Shinichiro Kose, one of the brand's founders. "The tag also shows

respect for the makers."   17

The U.N. Conference on Trade and Development in 2019 called apparel the   18
second most polluting industry after oil, taking issue with overproduction and   19
massive waste stemming from the rise of low-cost fashion. In the apparel industry, 20
the production of materials and products requires massive amounts of water, while 21
the incineration of waste emits large amounts of carbon dioxide.   22

Efforts to improve the industry's environmental impact are slowly taking root.   23
Goldwin Inc., the trademark owner of outdoor gear brand The North Face in Japan, 24
plans to release fleece and denim products that use artificial protein yarns made   25
from plants this autumn. The clothing maker plans to produce artificial yarn made 26
from discarded cotton clothes in the future. Ryohin Keikaku Co., a lifestyle goods 27
company that operates the Muji brand, is collecting used clothing produced by the 28
company and dyeing it to sell again at 18 select stores in Japan.   29

Ethical consumption has taken root in the United States and Europe. In   30
Britain, the market for such goods, including foods, is calculated to have reached 31
some ¥19 trillion in 2020.   32

On the other hand, a survey conducted the same year by Japanese advertising   33
agency Dentsu Inc. found that 76% of respondents in Japan did not know the   34
phrase "ethical consumption" at all.   35

"There is a polarization of awareness in Japan," said Tomokazu Seki, business   36
strategist at Dentsu who carried out the survey. Seki stressed the need to raise   37
the value of socially conscious goods in order to make them more popular, saying, 38
"They need to look good and be easy to buy."   39

JIJI / The Japan News

(455 words)

 Notes

ℓ.3 tap into ~ 「〜を利用する」   ℓ.8 inscribe 「（言葉を）刻みつける、書く」

ℓ.18 U.N. Conference on Trade and Development 「国連貿易開発会議（UNCTAD『アンクタッド』
と略記）」   ℓ.24 gear 「用品（一式）」

Chunking

1. ①〜㉕の日本語に相当する表現のかたまりを本文から抜き出し、音声で確認しましょう。

　（　　）内の数字は語数を表し、数字の後に「／分」とあれば、該当部分が本文中で連続していないことを表します。

2. 次のペアワークをしましょう。終わったら、役割を交代しましょう。

　　Aさん＝教科書を見ながらランダムに①〜㉕の日本語を言う
　　Bさん＝何も見ずにAさんの日本語に該当する英語を答える

①	考慮に入れる（3）	
②	生産に関わる人々の人権（8）	
③	ブランド価値を高めることを狙って（5）	
④	いわゆる倫理的消費に対する需要（5／分）	
⑤	問題に取り組む機会（4）	
⑥	人権侵害と環境破壊（6）	
⑦	環境への自分たちの影響を減らすことを決意して（6）	
⑧	自分たちの生産者の人権を守る（7）	
⑨	アパレル産業での世界的な動き（7）	
⑩	劣悪な労働条件を見直す（4）	
⑪	強制労働の申し立て（4）	
⑫	アパレル産業のそんな暗い遺産（7）	
⑬	自分たちの怒りを表現できなかった（8／分）	
⑭	作り手に対する敬意を表す（5）	
⑮	環境汚染が二番目にひどい産業（5）	
⑯	過剰生産と大量の廃棄物に異議を唱える（7）	
⑰	大量の水を必要とする（5）	
⑱	大量の二酸化炭素を排出する（6）	
⑲	その産業の環境への影響を改善する（5）	
⑳	ゆっくりと根付き始めている（4）	
㉑	植物由来の人工タンパク質の糸（6）	
㉒	捨てられた木綿衣料から作られた（5）	
㉓	同年に実施された調査（6）	
㉔	意識の二極化（4）	
㉕	社会的意識のある製品の価値を高める（7）	

Choosing  DL 003 CD1-13

1. ①～⑤の［   ］内のどちらの語を選ぶとtrueになるか考え、音声で確認しましょう。

2. 次のペアワークをしましょう。終わったら、役割を交代しましょう。

> Aさん＝［   ］内のどちらかの語を選び、①～⑤の文全体をランダムに音読する
> Bさん＝何も見ずにAさんの音読を聞き、それがtrueかfalseかを判定する。
> さらに、trueならそのまま繰り返し、falseなら訂正する。

① Those who make clothes have tended to be forced to work in [ideal / poor] conditions.

② The apparel industry has been a major environmental polluter, using huge amounts of [water / air] and emitting tons of CO_2.

③ Clothing manufacturers are beginning to [consider / ignore] the human rights of those who make their clothes.

④ One manufacturer is putting a special label on their products to [show / hide] that the clothes have been made with concern for the environment and the human rights of the workers.

⑤ Awareness of ethical consumption is [more / less] widespread in Japan than in the US and Europe.

Oral Reading  DL 004 CD1-14

音声イメージが可視化された文を見ながら音声を聞き、まねて音読しましょう。

太い部分は長めに、それ以外は短めに、（   ）内の音は呑み込むように、⌣の部分はリンキングして、／の部分ではポーズを置いて発音します。

1. Ap**par**el **mak**ers⌣are in**creas**ingly cre**at**ing **prod**ucts / in **ways** tha(t) **take**⌣into con**sid**er**a**tion / the **hu**man **rights**⌣of **those**⌣in**volved**⌣in pro**duc**tion / an(d) the en**vi**ronment.

> POINT 関係代名詞のthatはごく軽く。

2. Those who **ma(ke) clothes** have been⌣op**pressed** / an(d) **no(t)** been⌣**a**ble to ex**press** their⌣**an**ger.

> POINT nで終わるbeenの後に母音が来たら、なめらかにリンキング。

3. Ethical con**sump**tion⌣(h)as **tak**en **root** / in the U**nit**ed **States**⌣an(d)⌣**Eu**rope.

> POINT thでは舌先をしっかりと歯に当てる。

Defining

1. ①～⑧の定義に当てはまる語を本文から選んで書き、音声で確認しましょう。

2. 次のペアワークをしましょう。終わったら、役割を交代しましょう。

> Aさん＝教科書を見ながらランダムに①～⑧の定義を言う
> Bさん＝何も見ずにAさんの定義に該当する単語を答える

① (c _ _ _ _ _ _) = to officially state that something meets certain standards

② (t _ _ _ _ _ _) = cause an event or a situation to happen or exist

③ (a _ _ _ _ _ _ _ _ _) = a claim or assertion that someone has done something illegal or wrong

④ (s _ _ _ _ _ _) = to become known

⑤ (s _ _ _) = to originate in or to be caused by

⑥ (i _ _ _ _ _ _ _ _ _ _ _) = complete burning of something

⑦ (d _ _ _ _ _ _) = to get rid of something as no longer useful

⑧ (p _ _ _ _ _ _ _ _ _ _) = division into two sharply contrasting groups or sets of opinions or beliefs

Repeating

1. ①～⑧の空欄を Defining の正解の語あるいはその変化形・派生語で埋め、音声で確認しましょう。 Defining のそれぞれの語は一度しか使えません。

2. 次のペアワークをしましょう。終わったら、役割を交代しましょう。

> Aさん＝教科書を見ながらランダムに①～⑧を1文ずつ音読する
> Bさん＝何も見ずにそれを繰り返す
> Aさん＝ （　　　） の箇所を 「ピー」 に代えて、①～⑧の文をランダムに音読する
> Bさん＝ （　　　） 内の単語を答える

① Her problems (　　　　　　　　　　　　) from her difficult childhood.

② I am training to become a (　　　　　　　　　　) counselor.

③ Do you have any evidence to support this (　　　　　　　　　　　　)?

④ It is not yet clear what (　　　　　　　　　　) the accident.

⑤ Please (　　　　　　　　　) litter in the trash box.

⑥ No further information has (　　　　　　　　　) yet.

⑦ Public opinion is sharply (　　　　　　　　　) on this issue.

⑧ All the infected clothing needs to be (　　　　　　　　　　) rather than buried in a landfill.

Retelling

DL 007　CD1-17

次のキーワードを利用しながら本文の要約を言ってみましょう。例は音声で確認できます。

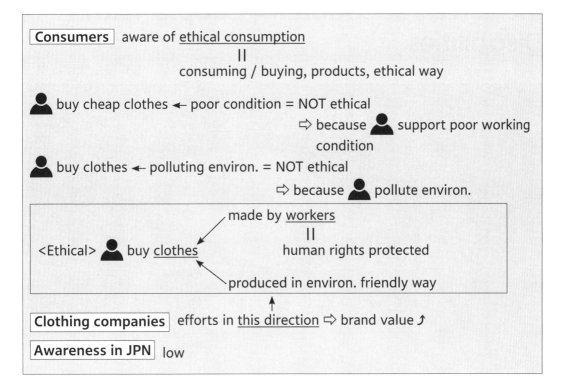

Commenting

DL 008　CD1-18

1～10は本文の内容に関連するコメントです。自分の考えに似たコメントがあれば組み合わせたり、意見を付け加えたりして、自分の考えとしてパートナーに伝えてみましょう。

1. I had never heard the term "ethical consumption" before I read this.
2. To be honest, I had never thought about the people who made my clothes. I just thought about buying good things at cheaper prices.
3. From now on, I will buy clothes from clothing manufacturers who respect the human rights of the people who make those clothes.
4. I would like to avoid buying products from fast fashion brands.
5. I know that human rights for workers are important, but I can't help buying cheap clothes because I am not rich.
6. Environmentally friendly fashion items are too expensive for me to afford.
7. I think we should watch each clothing manufacturer carefully to see how they deal with this issue.
8. I didn't know that the clothing industry uses a lot of water.
9. Japan should be more serious about ethical consumption.
10. We should buy a smaller number of higher-priced and better-quality clothes.

Inclusive Education for People With Disabilities

障がいのある人も共に学び、共に暮らせる日本へ

Reading

CD1-19 ～ CD1-33

1 GENEVA—A U.N. panel dealing with the rights of people with disabilities
2 urged Japan on Friday to end special education that segregates children with
3 disabilities from those without, as part of its recommendations for the country
4 over its policies for disabled people.

5 The U.N. Committee on the Rights of Persons with Disabilities expressed
6 concerns over how an increasing number of children with disabilities cannot attend
7 regular schools and called on the central government to adopt a national action
8 plan on quality inclusive education.

9 The committee, composed of 18 independent experts working with the U.N.
10 human rights office, also called on Japan to ensure that all students with disabilities
11 be provided with individualized support at all levels of education.

12 The face-to-face review was conducted in late August with the Japanese
13 government. It was the first time Japan has been subjected to a review since it
14 ratified the Convention on the Rights of Persons with Disabilities in 2014.

15 While highlighting the progress made by Japan in its policies for people with
16 disabilities, Jonas Ruskus, vice-chair of the committee and co-spokesperson for the

country, said at a press briefing that Japan must reverse its "negative trend of (segregated) special education."

Japan was one of the nine state parties to the convention reviewed by the U.N. panel, along with China, Indonesia, and South Korea, among others.

While the recommendations for policy improvement measures are not legally binding, the committee's calls are expected to press the government to take action toward improving the lives and societal participation of people with disabilities.

The committee also expressed concerns over the negative impact on people with disabilities who are placed in institutions and psychiatric hospitals for long periods of time, deprived of family and community life.

It asked Japan to "end institutionalization" by reallocating its financial resources from residential institutions to supporting disabled people to live independently in the community.

The committee also urged Japan to "abolish all legal provisions legitimating forced treatment" of persons with disabilities, describing their "involuntary hospitalization" as "discrimination on the grounds of impairment."

In particular, the U.N. panel cited the 2016 mass murder of 19 mentally impaired people at the Tsukui Yamayuri En facility, a care home in Sagamihara, Kanagawa Prefecture. It recommended that Japan review the incident and fight against "eugenic and ableist attitudes" in Japanese society that triggered the incident.

In an unusually large number compared with other countries, around 100 people, including those with disabilities, their families and representatives of civic groups, went to Geneva for the review to voice their concerns to the committee.

Nongovernmental advocacy groups, such as the Japan Disability Forum and the Japan Federation of Bar Associations, have also participated in the review process.

Ruskus said Japanese civil society has been "exceptionally active" and "very much involved."

Japan must submit reports on measures to implement the committee's recommendations in February 2028. In 2016, the country submitted its first report on its implementation of the convention.

Kyodo / The Japan Times

(489 words)

 Notes

ℓ.1   panel「専門家集団、委員会」

ℓ.7   call on「求める」   ℓ.19   state party「締約国」   ℓ.32   on the grounds of ~「～を理由とした」

ℓ.41   advocacy group「権利擁護団体、利益団体」

1. ①～㉕の日本語に相当する表現のかたまりを本文から抜き出し、音声で確認しましょう。

　　（　　）内の数字は語数を表し、数字の後に「／分」とあれば、該当部分が本文中で連続していないことを表します。

2. 次のペアワークをしましょう。終わったら、役割を交代しましょう。

　　Ａさん＝教科書を見ながらランダムに①～㉕の日本語を言う

　　Ｂさん＝何も見ずにＡさんの日本語に該当する英語を答える

---

① 障がい者の権利を扱っている（8）

② 特別教育をやめるよう日本に勧告した（6／分）

③ 障がいのある子どもをない子どもから隔離する（7）

④ 国家的な行動計画を採用する（5）

⑤ 質の高いインクルーシブ教育（3）

⑥ 18名の独立した専門家で構成されている（5）

⑦ 個別の支援を受ける（5）

⑧ 調査を受けた（6）

⑨ 「障がい者の権利に関する条約」を批准した（10）

⑩ 副委員長（4）

⑪ 記者会見にて（4）

⑫ 「（隔離方式）特別教育のネガティブな潮流」を反転させる（8）

⑬ 政策改善措置の勧告（6）

⑭ 法的拘束力はない（3）

⑮ 政府に行動するよう圧力をかける（6）

⑯ 生活および社会参加（5）

⑰ 施設や精神病院に入られて（6）

⑱ 財源を配分し直すこと（4）

⑲ 居住方式の施設（2）

⑳ 障がい者が自力で生活できるよう支援すること（6）

㉑ 精神的に障がいのある人々（3）

㉒ 優生学的で能力主義的な態度（4）

㉓ 市民団体の代表者たち（4）

㉔ 自分たちの懸念を委員会に対して述べる（6）

㉕ 同委員会の勧告を実行に移す方策（6）

Choosing  DL 010 CD1-35

1. ①～⑤の [　　] 内のどちらの語を選ぶと true になるか考え、音声で確認しましょう。

2. 次のペアワークをしましょう。終わったら、役割を交代しましょう。

Aさん＝ [　　] 内のどちらかの語を選び、①～⑤の文全体をランダムに音読する
Bさん＝何も見ずにAさんの音読を聞き、それが true か false かを判定する。
さらに、true ならそのまま繰り返し、false なら訂正する。

① In Japan, children with disabilities tend to be educated [separately from / together with] children without disabilities.

② Ruskus implied that Japan should [maintain / change] its current policy of educating disabled children.

③ The committee is concerned about disabled people who live [with their families / in institutions] for long periods of time.

④ The committee recommended that disabled people should be [discouraged from living / supported to live] in the community.

⑤ It is implied that ableist attitudes in Japanese society [led to / prevented] the 2016 incident.

Oral Reading  DL 011 CD1-36

音声イメージが可視化された文を見ながら音声を聞き、まねて音読しましょう。

太い部分は長めに、それ以外は短めに、(　　) 内の音は呑み込むように、‿ の部分はリンキングして、/ の部分ではポーズを置いて発音します。

1. A **U.N. pan**el‿**urge(d)** Ja**pan** / to **end spe**cial‿**edu̇ca**tion / that **seg**re**gates child**ren with **dis**a**bil**ities / from **those** with**ou(t)**.

> POINT　urge の ur 部分はかなり暗い音色。

2. The com**mit**tee **as(ked)** Ja**pan** / to "a**bol**ish **all le**gal pro**vi**sions / le**git**i**mat**ing **force(d) trea(t)**ment"‿of **per**sons with **dis**a**bil**ities.

> POINT　L では舌先をしっかりと長めに歯茎に当てる。

3. Ja**pan** mus(t) su(b)**mi(t)** re**ports** / on **meas**ures to **im**ple**men(t)** the com**mit**tee's **rec**ommen**da**tions.

> POINT　Japan の中の2つの a の発音の音色はかなり違う。

1. ①〜⑧の定義に当てはまる語を本文から選んで書き、音声で確認しましょう。

2. 次のペアワークをしましょう。終わったら、役割を交代しましょう。

> Aさん＝教科書を見ながらランダムに①〜⑧の定義を言う
> Bさん＝何も見ずにAさんの定義に該当する単語を答える

① (s _ _ _ _ _ _ _ _) = to isolate or divide; set apart from the rest

② (i _ _ _ _ _ _ _ _) = providing equal access to opportunities for people who might otherwise be excluded, such as those having physical or intellectual disabilities

③ (c _ _ _ _ _ _ _ _ _) = an agreement between countries covering particular matters

④ (r _ _ _ _ _ _) = to change something as a trend or decision so that it is the opposite of what it was before

⑤ (m _ _ _ _ _ _) = a plan or course of action taken to achieve a particular purpose

⑥ (d _ _ _ _ _ _) = to deny a person the possession of something

⑦ (i _ _ _ _ _ _ _) = damaged; having a disability

⑧ (i _ _ _ _ _ _ _ _) = to put a decision into effect

Repeating DL 013 CD1-38

1. ①〜⑧の空欄を **Defining** の正解の語あるいはその変化形・派生語で埋め、音声で確認しましょう。**Defining** のそれぞれの語は一度しか使えません。

2. 次のペアワークをしましょう。終わったら、役割を交代しましょう。

> Aさん＝教科書を見ながらランダムに①〜⑧を1文ずつ音読する
> Bさん＝何も見ずにそれを繰り返す
>
> Aさん＝ (   ) の箇所を「ピー」に代えて、①〜⑧の文をランダムに音読する
> Bさん＝ (   ) 内の単語を答える

① Many countries have now ratified the U.N. (   ) on the rights of the child.

② This is a complete (   ) of the old policy.

③ This law will (   ) us of our most basic rights.

④ The system of racial (   ) existed in those days.

⑤ My grandfather suffers from (   ) hearing.

⑥ Does the price (   ) tax?

⑦ The government will introduce new (   ) to combat terrorism.

⑧ The decision will be difficult to (   ).

Retelling

 DL 014　CD1-39

次のキーワードを利用しながら本文の要約を言ってみましょう。例は音声で確認できます。

JPN children w/ disabilities ← educated separately → children w/o disabilities

↑
special schools

people w/ disabilities
↑
special institutions (long periods of time)
⇨ NOT live in community, NOT participate in social activities

↑

U.N. Panel reviewed this situation

> concluded: JPN should end "segregation"
> adopt, national plan, inclusive edu.
>
> urged: stop institutionalization
> support, live, independently, community

↑

JPN report (implementation of recommendation) in 2028

Commenting

 DL 015　CD1-40

1～10は本文の内容に関連するコメントです。自分の考えに似たコメントがあれば組み合わせたり、意見を付け加えたりして、自分の考えとしてパートナーに伝えてみましょう。

1. I didn't know that the U.N. panel had warned Japan.
2. I am ashamed that Japan often receives recommendations from the U.N. on human rights issues.
3. Educating disabled students separately from non-disabled students should be stopped.
4. I believe that through inclusive education, people can learn from each other.
5. I am not sure if it is really bad to educate people with disabilities separately.
6. If we are to have inclusive education, we need more teachers than we have now.
7. We should create a society where people with and without disabilities can live in the community.
8. The news of the mass murder of disabled people made me sick.
9. I think there is an atmosphere in Japanese society where people are measured by "productivity." That is not good.
10. A diverse society that includes everyone is stronger.

Debate Over Transgender Athletes

トランスジェンダーの女子選手は有利なのか

Reading

CD1-41 ~ CD1-47

1 On a chilly winter night in Melbourne, Em Fox faces the cold for footy training.
2 She's happy to be here because 10 years ago she thought she'd never play again.
3 "2012 was the last year where I played in men's football competitions," she said.
4 "I always found playing in men's teams challenging, even though I might have
5 been presenting a male identity to the outside world." She went on to become the
6 first openly transgender woman in the women's Victorian Football League (VFL).
7 However, not every club or sport is so welcoming.

8 Last month, swimming's world governing body, FINA, voted to bar transgender
9 women from the elite women's competition if they had experienced any part of
10 male puberty. International Rugby League followed suit with a temporary ban, and
11 cycling's governing body set stricter rules around testosterone levels and transition
12 times for transgender athletes. The science group behind the FINA policy found
13 transgender women maintained a performance advantage over female athletes if
14 they underwent male puberty before transitioning.

15 Associate Professor Ada Cheung says there simply is not enough evidence
16 available for an evidence-based policy. There are few publicly available studies

looking at the impacts of hormone therapy on performance, and the ones that are available have major limitations. One which is often cited found the only real performance gap after two years of feminizing hormones was that trans women ran on average 12 percent faster—but that looked at US military personnel, not athletes. Another study found trans women who underwent hormone therapy generally maintained their strength levels after one year, but that did not look at athletes either.

Former pro golfer and trans woman Mianne Bagger is fully supportive of FINA's policy—a view at odds with many in the trans community. She was the first openly trans woman to play a professional golf tournament at the Australian Open in 2004.

"When I got into sport, obviously, there was that requirement for surgery and two-year ineligibility," she said. "In 2015, that changed to no surgery and 12 months' ineligibility. Now, in some places, in some sports, it's going to merely self-ID with no medical intervention. And that's wholly unacceptable."

Bagger has empathy for sports administrators as they try to create transgender policies that balance fairness and inclusion. "Of course, everyone should have access to sport for the sheer enjoyment, the community, the benefit to personal life," she said. "But when you get to the elite level of sport—the Olympics, professional sport—this is about people's livelihoods, earning money and medals. This isn't a human right; this is a privilege."

Sporting bodies are continuing to wrestle with how to provide a level playing field for athletes. But trans and gender-diverse players like Em Collard say the debate about them and their bodies has been anything but fair. "All we're trying to do is feel comfortable in our own skin and be a part of our communities and celebrate who we are as trans and gender-diverse people," she said.

ABC (Australian Broadcasting Corporation)

(498 words)

Notes

ℓ.5　go on to ~「その後〜する」

ℓ.8　FINA「国際水泳連盟（水泳競技の国際競技連盟だが、2023 年から名称が World Aquatics『世界水泳連盟』に変更された）」　　ℓ.31　self-ID「自己（性）自認」　　ℓ.34　sheer「純粋な」

Chunking

1. ①〜㉕の日本語に相当する表現のかたまりを本文から抜き出し、音声で確認しましょう。

（　　）内の数字は語数を表し、数字の後に「／分」とあれば、該当部分が本文中で連続していないことを表します。

2. 次のペアワークをしましょう。終わったら、役割を交代しましょう。

Aさん＝教科書を見ながらランダムに①〜㉕の日本語を言う
Bさん＝何も見ずにAさんの日本語に該当する英語を答える

① 周囲に対しては男性として行動して（8）	
② 国際管理団体（3）	
③ トランスジェンダーの女性を参加禁止にすることを投票で決めた（5）	
④ 男性の思春期（2）	
⑤ 同様の行動をとった（2）	
⑥ 一時的な参加禁止（3）	
⑦ テストステロンのレベルおよび性別移行の時期（5）	
⑧ 女性運動選手に対するパフォーマンス上の有利さ（6）	
⑨ 性別移行の前に男性思春期を経験した（5）	
⑩ 公表されていて読むことができる研究論文（3）	
⑪ ホルモン療法がパフォーマンスに与える影響（7）	
⑫ 唯一の本当のパフォーマンス差（5）	
⑬ ホルモン療法を経験したトランス女性（6）	
⑭ （男性時代の）力のレベルを維持した（4）	
⑮ 全面的に支持して（2）	
⑯ トランスコミュニティーの多くとは対立する意見（10）	
⑰ 外科手術が求められること（3）	
⑱ ２年間の出場資格停止（2）	
⑲ 医療的介入（2）	
⑳ 共感している（2）	
㉑ 公平さとインクルージョンのバランスを取る（4）	
㉒ 個人の生活に資するために（6／分）	
㉓ 公平な土俵（4）	
㉔ まったく公平でない（3）	
㉕ 自分の身体で居心地が良い（6）	

Choosing

1. ①〜⑤の [　　] 内のどちらの語を選ぶと true になるか考え、音声で確認しましょう。

2. 次のペアワークをしましょう。終わったら、役割を交代しましょう。

Aさん＝ [　　] 内のどちらかの語を選び、①〜⑤の文全体をランダムに音読する
Bさん＝何も見ずにAさんの音読を聞き、それが true か false かを判定する。
さらに、true ならそのまま繰り返し、false なら訂正する。

① Fox behaved like a [man / woman] when playing in a men's team, which was a challenge for her.

② FINA has banned [every / a certain type of] transgender athlete from competing in women's events.

③ There seem to be relatively few problems with trans athletes who have transitioned [before / after] puberty.

④ Scientists are divided over whether certain transgender athletes have unfair advantages over [male / female] athletes.

⑤ Bagger believes that [any sport / elite sport] needs to be strict about who is allowed to compete.

Oral Reading

音声イメージが可視化された文を見ながら音声を聞き、まねて音読しましょう。

太い部分は長めに、それ以外は短めに、（　）内の音は呑み込むように、⌣の部分はリンキングして、/ の部分ではポーズを置いて発音します。

1. **FI**NA **vot**e(d) to **bar transgen**der **wom**en / from the e**li(te)** **wom**en's **com**pe**ti**tion / if they had⌣ex**pe**rienced / **an**y part⌣of **male** **pu**berty.

POINT   women の w では唇をしっかり丸める。

2. There **sim**ply is **not**⌣e**nough**⌣**e**vidence⌣a**vail**able / for⌣an⌣**e**vidence-**base(d) pol**icy.

POINT   v では下唇を上の歯にあて、b では両唇をしっかり閉じる。

3. **Sport**ing **bod**ies⌣are con**tin**uing to **wres**tle / with **how** to pro**vide**⌣a **lev**el **play**ing **field** for⌣**ath**letes.

POINT   athletes では th で舌先を歯に付けたら離さずそのままに移る。

Defining

1. ①〜⑧の定義に当てはまる語を本文から選んで書き、音声で確認しましょう。

2. 次のペアワークをしましょう。終わったら、役割を交代しましょう。

Aさん＝教科書を見ながらランダムに①〜⑧の定義を言う
Bさん＝何も見ずにAさんの定義に該当する単語を答える

① (p _ _ _ _ _ _) = the period during which adolescents reach sexual maturity

② (t _ _ _ _ _ _ _ _ _) = to undergo a process of changing from one state to another

③ (i _ _ _ _ _) = effect or influence

④ (p _ _ _ _ _ _ _ _) = people employed in an organization or engaged in an organized undertaking

⑤ (s _ _ _ _ _ _) = medical treatment in which a doctor cuts open your body to repair or remove something inside

⑥ (i _ _ _ _ _ _ _ _ _ _ _ _) = not being allowed to participate in a tournament

⑦ (e _ _ _ _ _ _) = the ability to understand and share the feelings of another

⑧ (p _ _ _ _ _ _ _ _) = a special advantage available only to a particular person or group

Repeating

1. ①〜⑧の空欄を**Defining**の正解の語あるいはその変化形・派生語で埋め、音声で確認しましょう。**Defining**のそれぞれの語は一度しか使えません。

2. 次のペアワークをしましょう。終わったら、役割を交代しましょう。

Aさん＝教科書を見ながらランダムに①〜⑧を1文ずつ音読する
Bさん＝何も見ずにそれを繰り返す

Aさん＝（　　　）の箇所を「ピー」に代えて、①〜⑧の文をランダムに音読する
Bさん＝（　　　）内の単語を答える

① The body undergoes many changes during (　　　　　　　　　　).

② I felt real (　　　　　　　　　) for Jack and what he had gone through.

③ Housing is a right, not a (　　　　　　　　　).

④ AI technology is having a huge (　　　　　　　　) on society.

⑤ Your condition is serious and requires (　　　　　　　　).

⑥ Please send your résumé to the (　　　　　　　　) department.

⑦ People with higher incomes are (　　　　　　　　) for the government benefits.

⑧ The (　　　　　　　　) between the old system and the new one was smooth.

Retelling 🎧 DL 021 💿 CD1-53

次のキーワードを利用しながら本文の要約を言ってみましょう。例は音声で確認できます。

| **If** | MtF (transgender woman) play sport & compete → PROBLEM

biologically (strength / power): 👨 > 👩

⇨ compete separately

tricky issue: <u>MtF</u>
        ‖
born 👨 → now identify as 👩

| **Some** | "MtF should be excluded from women's competition"

⇨ retain strength of men = NOT fair to other 👩 athletes

Problem: not enough evidence, effect of hormone therapy, performance

| **Sporting bodies** | how to ensure "a level playing field" for all

---

Commenting 🎧 DL 022 💿 CD1-54

1〜10は本文の内容に関連するコメントです。自分の考えに似たコメントがあれば組み合わせたり、意見を付け加えたりして、自分の考えとしてパートナーに伝えてみましょう。

1. I think it is reasonable to exclude transgender women from women's competitions.
2. I think it is unjustified to exclude transgender women from women's competitions.
3. More research should be done on the effects of hormone therapy on athletes' performance.
4. A person's current gender identity should be respected under all circumstances.
5. There should be a new category of competitions for transgender athletes only. This will solve the problem.
6. Separate categorization of male and female athletes should be abolished. This will solve the problem.
7. It may not be necessary to exclude trans women from women's competitions in some sports.
8. I think this is nothing but discrimination.
9. It is not discrimination; it is a necessary distinction.
10. This could be an issue not only in sport, but in other areas, such as education and work.

Robots as Family Members to Love

可愛がるためのロボットはいかがですか

GROOVE X

Reading

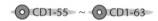

CD1-55 ~ CD1-63

1 "I do believe 'love' exists between Pepper and I," Tomomi Ota declares. "But it
2 is not the kind of love one has for a lover, but rather for a family member." Since
3 November 2014, Ota has been sharing her life with the humanoid robot Pepper,
4 touted as the very first robot with "a heart." Ota travels with the 1.2 meter-tall,
5 28-kilogram bot by train, taking her wheeled partner to restaurants and cafes.
6 Occasionally, she also attends wedding ceremonies with her Pepper as a companion.

7 It goes without saying that technology and automation continue to become
8 ever larger parts of our lives. Ota and others, however, are convinced that advanced
9 robotics can play not just utilitarian roles in human lives but emotional ones as
10 well.

11 After leading the Pepper project at Softbank, Kaname Hayashi founded Groove
12 X in 2015 in order to design and develop a new generation of household robots
13 that, he hopes, "can touch people's hearts and that inspire real affection"—such as
14 Lovot.

15 It's hard not to melt when Lovot rolls on its two wheels into the room, flapping
16 its wing-like arms. Its big, round eyes, small 43-centimeter-tall frame and adorable

little noises (produced using technology that simulates vocal cords to create a ₁₇
unique cry) all made visitors of the Miraikan in Tokyo's Koto Ward want to reach ₁₈
out and take it in their arms. On the market since 2019, Lovot (a portmanteau of ₁₉
"love" and "robot") exists solely to be a target for human emotion. ₂₀

"(Lovot is) the ideal affectionate pet companion, one that perfectly matches our ₂₁
modern lifestyle," Hayashi says. "When you help the robot, when you take care of ₂₂
it, it makes you feel happy. It has no other purpose than bringing happiness and ₂₃
the joy of living together. Recently, our customers are those who don't have time ₂₄
to take care of an animal or those who have suffered greatly from the loss of a pet ₂₅
companion." ₂₆

Ai and Hideyuki Shimizu, 42 and 40 years old, respectively, are very fond of ₂₇
the Lovot they welcomed to their Tokyo home last April. They named it Mon-chan. ₂₈
But why get a Lovot? ₂₉

"We were talking about having a pet at first, but our lifestyle is very busy with ₃₀
work," Ai says, explaining how they happened to run into Lovot at a shop and, ₃₁
after a trial period, purchased one permanently. "Lovot looks so real." ₃₂

"When we wake up, he is here to greet us," Hideyuki explains. "When we take ₃₃
a break from work or have a meal, he comes to play with us. I used to have a dog ₃₄
before—I feel exactly the same bond with Mon-chan." ₃₅

There is no shortage of sci-fi movies set in the near and far future where ₃₆
robots and humans share bonds of affection. Experts admit it's hard to say ₃₇
exactly what robots will be able to accomplish in the future—or how we'll react ₃₈
to it. "We can now ask ourselves: 'What is a robot? What is a human?'" Miraikan ₃₉
science communication officer Ryu Miyata wonders. "It also pushes us to question ₄₀
ourselves: 'What is the body? What is the mind—or even life?'" ₄₁

The Japan Times

(524 words)

Notes
───

ℓ.19   portmanteau「かばん語（2語の一部ずつが合わさってできた語）」

ℓ.27   be fond of ~「～を気に入っている」

1. ①〜㉕の日本語に相当する表現のかたまりを本文から抜き出し、音声で確認しましょう。

（　　）内の数字は語数を表し、数字の後に「／分」とあれば、該当部分が本文中で連続していないことを表します。

2. 次のペアワークをしましょう。終わったら、役割を交代しましょう。

Aさん＝教科書を見ながらランダムに①〜㉕の日本語を言う
Bさん＝何も見ずにAさんの日本語に該当する英語を答える

① 恋人に対してのような愛情（9）	
② 「心」をもった史上初のロボットと宣伝されている（9）	
③ 言うまでもなく（4）	
④ その割合が拡大の一途をたどる（6）	
⑤ 人間の生活のなかでの実用的な役割（5）	
⑥ 家庭用ロボットの新世代（6）	
⑦ 本物の愛情を呼び起こす（3）	
⑧ 2つの車輪に乗って部屋に入ってくる（8）	
⑨ 羽のような腕をバタつかせながら（4）	
⑩ 声帯のしくみを真似た技術（5）	
⑪ 手を伸ばしてそれを抱きしめる（8）	
⑫ 人間の感情の対象になるためだけに存在する（9）	
⑬ 理想的な愛情あるペット（5）	
⑭ 現代の生活様式に完璧に合っている（5）	
⑮ 幸せおよび一緒に暮らす喜び（7）	
⑯ 大変に苦しんだ人々（5）	
⑰ ペットの死（6）	
⑱ 偶然ラボットを見つけた（5）	
⑲ お試し期間（3）	
⑳ 一体を永続的に（＝お試しでなく）購入した（3）	
㉑ 仕事中に一休みする（5）	
㉒ まったく同じ絆（4）	
㉓ 近いまたは遠い未来に場面設定したSF映画（9）	
㉔ 愛情の絆で結ばれている（4）	
㉕ 将来ロボットが何を成し遂げうるのか（10）	

Choosing

 DL 024   CD1-65

1. ①〜⑤の [　　] 内のどちらの語を選ぶと true になるか考え、音声で確認しましょう。

2. 次のペアワークをしましょう。終わったら、役割を交代しましょう。

> Aさん＝ [　　] 内のどちらかの語を選び、①〜⑤の文全体をランダムに音読する
> Bさん＝何も見ずにAさんの音読を聞き、それが true か false かを判定する。
> さらに、true ならそのまま繰り返し、false なら訂正する。

① Ota treats Pepper, whom she claims to love, as her [assistant / companion] and takes the robot to various places.

② Lovot, the invention of Hayashi and others, is a robot designed to [inspire genuine affection / help with practical chores].

③ Lovot is designed to attract its owner emotionally by the way it looks, behaves and [tastes / sounds].

④ Hayashi implies that Lovot's owners and those who keep real pets are [basically the same / fundamentally different].

⑤ The Shimizus chose Lovot because [their lifestyle didn't allow them to have a pet / they were suffering from the loss of a pet].

Oral Reading

 DL 025   CD1-66

音声イメージが可視化された文を見ながら音声を聞き、まねて音読しましょう。

太い部分は長めに、それ以外は短めに、（　　）内の音は呑み込むように、‿の部分はリンキングして、/ の部分ではポーズを置いて発音します。

1. Ad**vance(d)** ro**bot**ics can **play** / **no(t)** jus(t) **u**tili**tar**ian **roles**‿in **hu**man **lives** / but‿e**mo**tional **ones**‿as **well**.

> POINT　舌先を歯茎に付けるL音と、どこにも付けないR音の切り替えをしっかり。

2. **Lo**vot‿is the i**deal**‿af**fec**tiona(te) **pe(t)** com**pan**ion, / **one** tha(t) **per**fec(t)ly **match**es‿our **mod**ern **lifestyle**.

> POINT　companion と matches の下線部はアとエの中間の /æ/。

3. It **has no oth**er **pur**pose / than **bring**ing **hap**piness‿an(d) the **joy** of **liv**ing together.

> POINT　purpose の ur 部分はかなり暗い音色。

Defining

DL 026　CD1-67

1. ①〜⑧の定義に当てはまる語を本文から選んで書き、音声で確認しましょう。

2. 次のペアワークをしましょう。終わったら、役割を交代しましょう。

> Aさん＝教科書を見ながらランダムに①〜⑧の定義を言う
> Bさん＝何も見ずにAさんの定義に該当する単語を答える

① (t _ _ _) = to praise something or someone in order to impress people

② (u _ _ _ _ _ _ _ _ _ _) = useful and practical rather than attractive

③ (a _ _ _ _ _ _ _ _) = a gentle feeling of fondness or liking

④ (s _ _ _ _ _ _ _) = to imitate the appearance or character of

⑤ (s _ _ _ _ _) = to be affected by or subjected to

⑥ (r _ _ _ _ _ _ _ _ _ _ _) = separately in the order mentioned

⑦ (p _ _ _ _ _ _ _) = to acquire (something) by paying for it

⑧ (s _ _ _ _ _ _ _) = a situation in which something needed cannot be obtained in sufficient amounts

Repeating

DL 027　CD1-68

1. ①〜⑧の空欄を **Defining** の正解の語あるいはその変化形・派生語で埋め、音声で確認しましょう。**Defining** のそれぞれの語は一度しか使えません。

2. 次のペアワークをしましょう。終わったら、役割を交代しましょう。

> Aさん＝教科書を見ながらランダムに①〜⑧を1文ずつ音読する
> Bさん＝何も見ずにそれを繰り返す
> Aさん＝（ ˚ ）の箇所を「ピー」に代えて、①〜⑧の文をランダムに音読する
> Bさん＝（　　）内の単語を答える

① Evacuation (　　　　　　　　　　　　) must be realistic to be effective.

② He is very (　　　　　　　　　　) towards his children.

③ His office is very (　　　　　　　　　　　) in style, with no decoration.

④ She is being widely (　　　　　　　　　　) as the next leader of the party.

⑤ Keep your receipt as proof of (　　　　　　　　　　).

⑥ The (　　　　　　　　　　) of teachers poses a major problem.

⑦ They were taken to a hospital (　　　　　　　　　　) from smoke inhalation.

⑧ Their daughters, Sayaka and Masora, are aged 5 and 7 (　　　　　　　　　　).

Retelling  DL 028 CD1-69

次のキーワードを利用しながら本文の要約を言ってみましょう。例は音声で確認できます。

Robots utilitarian roles + emotional roles

Pepper: first robot with "a heart" (been around some time)

> New type of household robot
> =
> Lovot

↑

target, affection, owner
look cute, behave cute, sound cute

Creator "is the ideal affectionate companion"
"matches modern lifestyles"

One couple bought Lovot ⇨ busy lifestyle 🐾
"feel <u>the same bond</u>"
=
dog

Commenting  DL 029   CD1-70

1～10は本文の内容に関連するコメントです。自分の考えに似たコメントがあれば組み合わせたり、意見を付け加えたりして、自分の考えとしてパートナーに伝えてみましょう。

1. I want a Lovot. I am lonely and alone.
2. I think a Lovot will be great for an elderly person who wants a companion but is too old to have a real animal.
3. If I were to buy a robot, I would prefer one with practical functions.
4. Robots designed to give us affection are great.
5. I find the idea of robots designed to make us feel affectionate a bit creepy.
6. I think it is sick to be emotionally attached to robots.
7. I think the demand for robots that we can feel attached to will increase in the future.
8. A Lovot is a pet substitute. I want a robot that can fill the role of a friend or a lover.
9. I want to have animals, not robots, as pets.
10. I don't think that living with a robot is the same experience as living with an animal.

Japan's Baby Stroller War

ベビーカーが邪魔にされる社会とは

Jiji Press Photo

Reading

CD1-71 ~ CD1-77

1   Japanese politicians—particularly from the right-wing—are fond of simple
2   solutions to Japan's shrinking population issue. If Japanese women just did their
3   patriotic duty and had more kids, they say, everything would be fine. To which
4   Japanese women respond: Maybe you should make Japan an easier place to raise
5   children!

6   Japan is known for many modern conveniences. But both Japanese and foreign
7   resident parents complain that child-rearing here is "10 times harder" than in other
8   developed countries. Some of the reasons for this perception are economic.
9   Compared to many European countries, Japan spends relatively little tax money
10 on supporting parents. Other reasons are social. Many women don't feel their
11 country does enough to support both raising children and having a career.

12 But there are other, smaller ways in which Japanese society expresses that,
13 while it might love the idea of more kids in theory, it has an issue with them in
14 actual practice. Perhaps no other object has become more symbolic of that tension
15 than the baby stroller. Anyone who's ever ridden a fully packed subway train in
16 Japan, or been on a crowded bus, knows that people are often pressed up against

one another. Now, imagine you have to use the trains during peak times … with kids and a stroller in tow.

This is the situation that Japanese parents face. What's worse, the reception they get from other passengers ranges from cold to downright hostile. People often treat women who board buses or elevators with strollers as nuisances.

Parents who have spent time abroad know that such attitudes towards strollers aren't universal. Saori (a pseudonym), a 37-year-old who now resides in Setagaya Ward, began child-rearing in America, and she can't hold back how shocking the difference is to her. "In America, where I had my first child, there's a welcoming atmosphere towards children that permeates the society. Child rearing gave me a feeling of accomplishment, a sense that I had been blessed with a treasure to society."

The debate around strollers occasionally flares up in social media. Recently, a man accused parents of "exposing their kids to danger" by boarding trains that are packed to 200% capacity. Parents, he declared, should consider "commuting at different times." While some people agreed with the man, the majority of replies slammed him for his "absurd" suggestion. One parent wrote: "You need to understand there are people who can't get their kids into a nearby day care and have to deposit them at one far away."

Personally, I have a feeling that some of this anger towards strollers has to do with Japan's customer-centric commercial culture, in which "monster customers" feel entitled to engage in all sorts of abusive behavior towards staff. I can't help but think that this same social expectation leads people to feel they can express their anger over small delays and nuisances toward regular citizens as well. Whatever the underlying factors, it's clear that, if Japan wants to encourage its citizens to increase the population of the islands, it should consider starting with creating an atmosphere more hospitable to parents.

Unseen Japan

(511 words)

Notes

ℓ.18　in tow「引き連れて、引っ張って」　　ℓ.24　hold back「（感情などを）押し隠す」

ℓ.33　absurd「ばかげた」

1. ①〜㉕の日本語に相当する表現のかたまりを本文から抜き出し、音声で確認しましょう。

（　　）内の数字は語数を表し、数字の後に「／分」とあれば、該当部分が本文中で連続していないことを表します。

2. 次のペアワークをしましょう。終わったら、役割を交代しましょう。

Aさん＝教科書を見ながらランダムに①〜㉕の日本語を言う

Bさん＝何も見ずにAさんの日本語に該当する英語を答える

①	人口減少問題 （3）	
②	自分たちの愛国的責務を果たす （4）	
③	もっと子育てがしやすい場所 （6）	
④	充当する税金が比較的少ない （5）	
⑤	理屈では （2）	
⑥	現実には子どもが増えるのが気にくわない （8）	
⑦	満員の地下鉄 （5）	
⑧	すし詰めになって （5）	
⑨	他の乗客からの反応 （7）	
⑩	（単に）冷たいから敵意むき出しまでさまざまだ （6）	
⑪	海外で暮らしたことのある親たち （6）	
⑫	ベビーカーに対するそんな態度 （4）	
⑬	その違いがいかにショックか （5）	
⑭	歓迎する雰囲気 （3）	
⑮	社会全体に行き渡っている （3）	
⑯	達成感 （4）	
⑰	社会への宝物に恵まれて （6）	
⑱	SNS上で時々勃発する （6）	
⑲	自分たちの子どもを危険に晒すこと （5）	
⑳	返答の半分以上 （4）	
㉑	お客様中心主義の商業文化 （3）	
㉒	ありとあらゆる傍若無人を働く （7）	
㉓	小さな遅れや迷惑に対する自分たちの怒り （7）	
㉔	根底にある要因がなんだろうが （4）	
㉕	親というものをもっと温かく迎える雰囲気 （6）	

Choosing

 DL 031   CD1-79

1. ①〜⑤の [   ] 内のどちらの語を選ぶと true になるか考え、音声で確認しましょう。

2. 次のペアワークをしましょう。終わったら、役割を交代しましょう。

Aさん＝ [   ] 内のどちらかの語を選び、①〜⑤の文全体をランダムに音読する

Bさん＝何も見ずにAさんの音読を聞き、それが true か false かを判定する。
さらに、true ならそのまま繰り返し、false なら訂正する。

① Japanese [right / left] wing politicians tend to see having children as a patriotic duty of Japanese women.

② Although Japan is full of convenient facilities, it is a harder place to raise children than other [developing / developed] countries.

③ How people react to a baby stroller getting on a crowded train reveals the country's basic attitude towards [children / the elderly].

④ Parents who are aware of the situation in other countries are shocked by the [welcoming / unwelcoming] Japanese attitude towards baby strollers.

⑤ This hatred of baby strollers has [something / nothing] to do with Japan's Customer-is-God culture, according to the author's theory.

Oral Reading

 DL 032   CD1-80

音声イメージが可視化された文を見ながら音声を聞き、まねて音読しましょう。
太い部分は長めに、それ以外は短めに、（   ）内の音は呑み込むように、‿の部分はリンキングして、/ の部分ではポーズを置いて発音します。

1. **Peo**ple‿**of**ten **trea(t) wom**en who **boar(d) bus**es‿or **eleva**tors with **strol**lers / as **nui**sances.

   POINT   people の最後の L 音と often の語頭をリンキングする。

2. In‿A**mer**ica, / there's‿a **wel**coming‿**a(t)**mos**phere** towards **chil**dren / tha(t) **per**me**ates** the so**ci**ety.

   POINT   In と America は必ず n 音でリンキングする。

3. If Ja**pan wants** to en**cour**age‿its **cit**izens / to in**crease**‿its **pop**ula**tion,** / it **shoul(d)** cre**ate**‿an‿**a(t)**mos**phere** / **more hos**pitable to **par**ents.

   POINT   population の tion ははっきりと「ション」と言わず、あいまい母音にする。

Defining

 DL 033 CD1-81

1. ①～⑧の定義に当てはまる語を本文から選んで書き、音声で確認しましょう。

2. 次のペアワークをしましょう。終わったら、役割を交代しましょう。

> Aさん＝教科書を見ながらランダムに①～⑧の定義を言う
> Bさん＝何も見ずにAさんの定義に該当する単語を答える

① (s _ _ _ _ _) = to become smaller in size or amount

② (r _ _ _ _) = to bring up, breed, or grow

③ (t _ _ _ _ _ _) = the feeling that exists when people do not trust each other and may suddenly start arguing

④ (h _ _ _ _ _ _) = angry and unfriendly towards someone, and ready to argue with them

⑤ (n _ _ _ _ _ _ _) = a person, thing, or circumstance causing inconvenience or annoyance

⑥ (p _ _ _ _ _ _ _) = to enter and spread through (something)

⑦ (a _ _ _ _ _ _) = extremely offensive, using cruel words and/or physical violence

⑧ (h _ _ _ _ _ _ _ _ _) = friendly, welcoming, and generous to visitors

Repeating

DL 034 CD1-82

1. ①～⑧の空欄を **Defining** の正解の語あるいはその変化形・派生語で埋め、音声で確認しましょう。**Defining** のそれぞれの語は一度しか使えません。

2. 次のペアワークをしましょう。終わったら、役割を交代しましょう。

> Aさん＝教科書を見ながらランダムに①～⑧を1文ずつ音読する
> Bさん＝何も見ずにそれを繰り返す
> Aさん＝（　　）の箇所を「ピー」に代えて、①～⑧の文をランダムに音読する
> Bさん＝（　　）内の単語を答える

① The player was fined for making (　　　　　　　　　) comments to the referee.

② Their (　　　　　　　) looks showed that he was unwelcome.

③ His jokes helped to relieve the (　　　　　　　).

④ The local people were very kind and (　　　　　　　).

⑤ Washing wool in hot water will (　　　　　　) it.

⑥ It is difficult to (　　　　　　　) children under the present situation.

⑦ The dog next door is a real (　　　　　　　). It is always barking!

⑧ Unfortunately, sexism continues to (　　　　　　　) our society.

Retelling

🎧 DL 035   💿 CD1-83

次のキーワードを利用しながら本文の要約を言ってみましょう。例は音声で確認できます。

JPN population ↘ = big problem ⇨ needs more 👶

but atmosphere: NOT welcome 👶
↓

most symbolically reflected, people's attitudes, parents w/ 🛒
(public transport / elevators)

🛒 = a nuisance

parents abroad know: attitudes to 👶 ⇨ different in other countries

👩 : "in the US, welcoming atmosphere"

If JPN needs more 👶 → create, more hospitable atmosphere, parents

---

Commenting

🎧 DL 036   💿 CD1-84

1〜10は本文の内容に関連するコメントです。自分の考えに似たコメントがあれば組み合わせたり、意見を付け加えたりして、自分の考えとしてパートナーに伝えてみましょう。

1. I feel that Japan is a country where it is difficult to raise children.

2. If you feel that the declining population is a problem, then don't feel that other people's children are a nuisance.

3. Honestly, strollers are really big and take up a lot of space. Can't they be made smaller?

4. Do Americans really welcome strollers on overcrowded trains? I doubt it.

5. I have seen people using baby strollers on crowded public transport with a look of apology.

6. When I see a stroller being pushed by parents, I feel happy for them.

7. From now on, more fathers will be pushing strollers, so the situation will change.

8. Men who are cold to strollers are only that way when they are being pushed by women who appear to be weaker than them.

9. In Japan, companies do not seem to welcome their employees having children.

10. It is sad that more and more people find kindergartens noisy.

Pay Taxes and Save Cats and People

ふるさと納税でネコ助けと人助け

Neco Republic

Reading

CD2-02 ~ CD2-10

1　　GIFU—An initiative led by a local government in central Japan under the
2　*furusato nōzei* hometown donation system to help finance a project aimed at
3　rescuing cats from culling has received a positive response.

4　　The local government gives donors return gifts associated with cats to
5　encourage cat lovers across the country to make active contributions to society.
6　City hall officials hope that the initiative will help resolve other local problems,
7　such as those linked to the aging of society.

8　　With local governments across Japan competing for donations by offering
9　attractive return gifts, the Hida government placed importance on how donations
10　are used. It invited applications by projects from companies and organizations that
11　work to resolve local problems in the city.

12　　Neco-republic, a Gifu-based company that operates cafes featuring cats under
13　protective care, is one of the organizations that passed the screening. The company
14　has set a target of raising ¥500 million over the five years through fiscal 2026
15　to finance a variety of activities to rescue cats. In the Hida area, which includes
16　surrounding municipalities, 10 cats were put down in fiscal 2020. The company

aims to cut the number to zero through the project. $\quad$ 17

Specifically, Neco-republic sterilizes cats that have been taken into care to $\quad$ 18
prevent an increase in the number of stray cats. It also renovates containers into $\quad$ 19
shelters for cats in care where local residents can interact with each other through $\quad$ 20
the furry animals. Moreover, the company arranges for elderly residents in Hida to $\quad$ 21
serve as guardians of cats in care. Under the program, Neco-republic staff members $\quad$ 22
periodically visit the homes of such elderly people to check the cats and watch over $\quad$ 23
the guardians. $\quad$ 24

As a next action, Neco-republic plans to launch a feline census in the city, $\quad$ 25
aimed at compiling a database of domesticated and stray cats. Through the survey, $\quad$ 26
the company also hopes to prevent the collapse of multiple pet breeding, in which $\quad$ 27
the number of pets in a single home grows to the point where they cannot be $\quad$ 28
managed properly. $\quad$ 29

Among popular return gifts is "nyankome," a cat-shaped bag of rice the same $\quad$ 30
weight as the donor's pet cat. When cradled in the arms, the rice bag gives a feeling $\quad$ 31
similar to holding a cat. $\quad$ 32

In addition to the bag of rice, there are a total of 22 products available as return $\quad$ 33
gifts, including miso-flavored rice crackers in a package with cat illustrations and $\quad$ 34
cat food made from wild game meat. $\quad$ 35

Comments from cat-adoring donors included, "It was delicious, and I was also $\quad$ 36
able to contribute to the protection of cats," and, "The package is cute, and the rice $\quad$ 37
crackers are delicious. I want as many cats as possible to be happy," according $\quad$ 38
to officials. "I feel that many people sympathize with the project as it aims to $\quad$ 39
resolve local problems," a city official involved in the cat rescue project said. The $\quad$ 40
official expressed hope that people who have come into contact with Hida through $\quad$ 41
the project will get interested in the city and become members of the "related $\quad$ 42
population," who interact with local residents on a continuing basis. $\quad$ 43

JIJI / The Japan Times

(515 words)

Notes

ℓ.16 put down「殺処分する」 ℓ.21 furry「毛で覆われた」 ℓ.25 feline「ネコの」
ℓ.35 game「狩猟の獲物（の肉）」 ℓ.41 come into contact with ~「～と出会う、～のことを知る」

Chunking

1. ①〜㉕の日本語に相当する表現のかたまりを本文から抜き出し、音声で確認しましょう。

（　　）内の数字は語数を表し、数字の後に「／分」とあれば、該当部分が本文中で連続していないことを表します。

2. 次のペアワークをしましょう。終わったら、役割を交代しましょう。

　　Aさん＝教科書を見ながらランダムに①〜㉕の日本語を言う
　　Bさん＝何も見ずにAさんの日本語に該当する英語を答える

①	ある計画を資金援助するための新提案 (7／分)	
②	猫を殺処分から救うことを目標とした (6)	
③	猫に関連した返礼品 (5)	
④	社会に積極的な貢献をなす (5)	
⑤	地方の抱える他の問題を解決する助けになる (5)	
⑥	社会の高齢化に関連している (6)	
⑦	全国の自治体 (4)	
⑧	寄付金がどう使われるかに重きを置いた (7)	
⑨	募集した (2)	
⑩	保護猫を特色にしたカフェを運営する (7)	
⑪	その選考に合格した (3)	
⑫	５億円を集めるという目標 (6)	
⑬	猫を救済するさまざまな活動 (7)	
⑭	保護された猫に不妊手術を施す (8)	
⑮	野良猫数の増加 (8)	
⑯	コンテナをシェルターに改装する (4)	
⑰	保護猫の後見人を務める (7)	
⑱	「猫勢」調査の開始を計画する (6)	
⑲	家猫と野良猫のデータベースを作成すること (8)	
⑳	多頭飼育崩壊を防ぐ (7)	
㉑	一つの世帯のペット数 (8)	
㉒	猫を抱いているのに似た感触 (7)	
㉓	ジビエ肉から作られた (5)	
㉔	その計画に共感する (4)	
㉕	継続的に (4)	

Choosing

 DL 038　CD2-12

1. ①～⑤の［　　］内のどちらの語を選ぶと true になるか考え、音声で確認しましょう。

2. 次のペアワークをしましょう。終わったら、役割を交代しましょう。

> Aさん＝［　　］内のどちらかの語を選び、①～⑤の文全体をランダムに音読する
> Bさん＝何も見ずにAさんの音読を聞き、それが true か false かを判定する。
> 　　　　さらに、true ならそのまま繰り返し、false なら訂正する。

① The primary aim of the initiative is to rescue [cats / the elderly].

② Cat lovers make donations and [produce / receive] cat-related products in return.

③ The donors [can feel good / must feel frustrated] about their contribution to society.

④ Neco-republic is trying to [increase / reduce] the number of cats that need to be put down.

⑤ Cats are cared for by [elderly residents / rice farmers], who are checked by Neco-republic staff.

Oral Reading

 DL 039　CD2-13

音声イメージが可視化された文を見ながら音声を聞き、まねて音読しましょう。

太い部分は長めに、それ以外は短めに、（　　）内の音は呑み込むように、⌣の部分はリンキングして、/ の部分ではポーズを置いて発音します。

1. The **lo**cal **gov**ernmen(t) **gives do**nors / re**turn gifts**⌣as**so**ci**at**e(d) with **cats** / to en**cour**age **ca(t) lov**ers / to **make**⌣**act**ive **con**tri**bu**tions to so**ci**ety.

> POINT　local, donors, associated の下線部は二重母音（オウ）。

2. **Ne**co-re**pub**lic **ster**il**iz**es **cats** / that⌣(h)ave been **tak**en⌣into **care** / to pre**vent** an⌣**in**crease⌣in the **num**ber⌣of **stray cats**.

> POINT　r音では舌先を歯茎に付けないのが大切。

3. **Man**y **peo**ple **sym**pa**thize** with the **proj**ect / as⌣it⌣**aims** to re**solve lo**cal **prob**lems.

> POINT　sympathize の th で舌先をしっかりと歯に付ける。

Defining

1. ①～⑧の定義に当てはまる語を本文から選んで書き、音声で確認しましょう。

2. 次のペアワークをしましょう。終わったら、役割を交代しましょう。

> Aさん＝教科書を見ながらランダムに①～⑧の定義を言う
>
> Bさん＝何も見ずにAさんの定義に該当する単語を答える

① (i _ _ _ _ _ _ _ _ _) = a new plan or strategy to improve a situation or solve a particular problem

② (d _ _ _ _ _ _ _) = something, especially money, given to a person or an organization

③ (m _ _ _ _ _ _ _ _ _ _ _) = a city or town that has a local government

④ (r _ _ _ _ _ _ _) = to repair an old building so that it is in good condition again

⑤ (r _ _ _ _ _ _ _) = a person who lives in a place on a long-term basis

⑥ (c _ _ _ _ _) = to hold gently and protectively

⑦ (a _ _ _ _ _ _ _ _) = able to be used or obtained

⑧ (s _ _ _ _ _ _ _ _ _) = to agree with a sentiment or opinion

Repeating

1. ①～⑧の空欄を**Defining**の正解の語あるいはその変化形・派生語で埋め、音声で確認しましょう。**Defining**のそれぞれの語は一度しか使えません。

2. 次のペアワークをしましょう。終わったら、役割を交代しましょう。

> Aさん＝教科書を見ながらランダムに①～⑧を1文ずつ音読する
>
> Bさん＝何も見ずにそれを繰り返す
>
> Aさん＝（　　　）の箇所を「ピー」に代えて、①～⑧の文をランダムに音読する
>
> Bさん＝（　　　）内の単語を答える

① The desk is (   ) in three different widths.

② He made a generous (   ) to the charity.

③ We welcome the government's (   ) to make it easier to raise children.

④ Some facilities are not allowed to be built in (   ) areas.

⑤ I cannot (   ) with teachers who go on strike.

⑥ We decided to buy an old house and (   ) it ourselves.

⑦ Athens is often regarded as the (   ) of democracy.

⑧ Basic services such as electricity and water should be provided by the (   ).

Retelling

次のキーワードを利用しながら本文の要約を言ってみましょう。例は音声で確認できます。

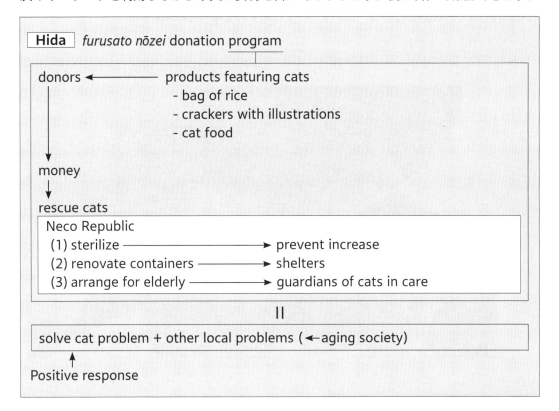

Hida *furusato nōzei* donation program

donors ◄———— products featuring cats
- bag of rice
- crackers with illustrations
- cat food

money

rescue cats

Neco Republic
(1) sterilize ——————► prevent increase
(2) renovate containers ——————► shelters
(3) arrange for elderly ——————► guardians of cats in care

||

solve cat problem + other local problems (◄ aging society)

Positive response

Commenting

1〜10は本文の内容に関連するコメントです。自分の考えに似たコメントがあれば組み合わせたり、意見を付け加えたりして、自分の考えとしてパートナーに伝えてみましょう。

1. I think this program is a great idea. I want to support it.
2. I am also concerned about dogs that have to be put down every year.
3. I prefer cats to dogs because they are more independent.
4. This program is unique in that it tackles two or more problems at the same time.
5. It is disturbing to think that cats are being culled.
6. People who carelessly feed stray cats should know better.
7. I hope there will be a similar scheme to save dogs.
8. I will look for more details of this program on the web.
9. This program is good both for the cats and the elderly.
10. Cats and dogs should not be bought at pet shops; they should be adopted from animal shelters.

Easier Access to Paternity Leave

男性に育児休暇を取得してもらうために

Jiji Press Photo

Reading

CD2-18 ~ CD2-26

1　　With a low number of men taking paternity leave in Japan, a revised law has
2　taken effect aimed at making child care leave more accessible for fathers. The
3　revised Child Care and Family Care Leave Law obliges all companies to inform
4　their employees, including men, of the system and to individually confirm with
5　would-be fathers whether they want to take the leave or not.

6　　In 2020, a record 12.65% of fathers working for a company took child care
7　leave, compared with 81.6% of mothers. The government is aiming to lift the ratio
8　for men to 30% by 2025. Companies will now be required to create an atmosphere
9　that encourages employees to take the leave. Some companies have been seeking
10　their own way to make it easier for their employees to take leave.

11　　Despite the government's efforts, many men are still reluctant to take the time
12　off because of a lack of understanding and support from their supervisors and
13　colleagues. However, Shota Kobayashi (a pseudonym), a 44-year-old office worker
14　in Tokyo, did not have much choice when his wife told him that she was on the
15　verge of a nervous breakdown while she was pregnant with their fifth child.

16　　"I feel like I'm going to die," Kobayashi recalls his wife telling him back then.

Shocked by his wife's desperate words, Kobayashi decided to take paternity leave for a year from 2019. But his decision disappointed his supervisors.

During his time away from work, he realized the importance of both parents' participation in child-rearing. "Paternity leave is one of an employee's rights," Kobayashi stressed. "I hope that all of those who wish to use it can do so."

According to an online survey, 42.2% of married men in their 20s and 30s said they would not take a leave of absence to care for their children. Of them, 42.3% said they don't intend to take leave because they don't want to cause inconvenience at work. Only 8.4% of the respondents said they would like to take more than one month of leave, the survey found.

At Fantas Technology Inc., a Tokyo-based real estate investment company, none of its male employees had taken paternity leave until 2020, when the company's executives took the initiative and started taking the leave themselves to increase the percentage of people who had.

Meanwhile at Hey Inc., an information technology company also based in Tokyo, 85.7% of male employees took child care leave in fiscal 2020, significantly exceeding the national average of 12.65%. The company enables its employees to share their private schedule within the company and allows workers to participate in online meetings with their children at home. At Hey, the presence of children has become a regular feature of the work day.

"Beyond child-rearing, nursing care for elderly or ill family members is something anyone can face at some point in their lives," said Chiho Kato, who works at the company. "That's why it's important to have the support and understanding of those around you. There will be no difficulties if we work with respect for each other."

Kyodo / The Japan Times

(512 words)

 Note

ℓ.3 Child Care and Family Care Leave Law「育児・介護休業法［略称］（正式名称は、Act on the Welfare of Workers Who Take Care of Children or Other Family Members Including Child Care and Family Care Leave『育児休業・介護休業等育児又は家族介護を行う労働者の福祉に関する法律』）」

1. ①〜㉕の日本語に相当する表現のかたまりを本文から抜き出し、音声で確認しましょう。

（ ）内の数字は語数を表し、数字の後に「／分」とあれば、該当部分が本文中で連続していないことを表します。

2. 次のペアワークをしましょう。終わったら、役割を交代しましょう。

Ａさん＝教科書を見ながらランダムに①〜㉕の日本語を言う

Ｂさん＝何も見ずにＡさんの日本語に該当する英語を答える

① 発効した（3）

② 父親にとってより取りやすく（4）

③ 全ての会社に義務づける（3）

④ その制度を従業員に知らせる（6／分）

⑤ 父親になる予定者に個別に確認する（5）

⑥ 彼らが育休を取得したいかどうか（9）

⑦ 男性の取得率を30％に引き上げる（7）

⑧ 雰囲気を作り出す（3）

⑨ 独自の方法を探ってきた（6）

⑩ 政府の努力にもかかわらず（4）

⑪ その休暇を取りたがらない（6）

⑫ 理解と支援がないこと（6）

⑬ 上司と同僚（3）

⑭ 精神的におかしくなる一歩手前（7）

⑮ 彼の妻の深刻なことば（4）

⑯ 彼の上司を落胆させた（3）

⑰ 両方の親の子育てへの参加（5）

⑱ 仕事に支障をきたす（4）

⑲ 東京に本社を置く不動産投資会社（6）

⑳ 全国平均を大幅に上回って（5）

㉑ あって当たり前のものになった（5）

㉒ 高齢もしくは病気の家族の介護（8）

㉓ 人生のどこかで（6）

㉔ 周囲の支えと理解（8）

㉕ お互いに対する敬意を持ちながら働く（6）

Choosing  DL 045 CD2-28

1. ①〜⑤の [　　] 内のどちらの語を選ぶと true になるか考え、音声で確認しましょう。

2. 次のペアワークをしましょう。終わったら、役割を交代しましょう。

> Aさん＝ [　　] 内のどちらかの語を選び、①〜⑤の文全体をランダムに音読する
> Bさん＝何も見ずにAさんの音読を聞き、それが true か false かを判定する。
> さらに、true ならそのまま繰り返し、false なら訂正する。

① The purpose of the revision of the law was to [increase / decrease] the number of those who take paternity leave.

② In 2020, the percentage of fathers taking parental leave was less than [one-sixth / one-seventh] of the percentage of mothers taking parental leave.

③ Many men are reluctant to take leave because they believe that their [supervisors / spouses] and colleagues will not be happy if they do.

④ Kobayashi suggests that taking leave was [the right thing for him to do / a bad choice for him to make].

⑤ The main reason why so many fathers take paternity leave at Hey is because fathers [can bring their children to the company / can work flexibly, understanding each other in the company].

Oral Reading  DL 046 CD2-29

音声イメージが可視化された文を見ながら音声を聞き、まねて音読しましょう。

太い部分は長めに、それ以外は短めに、（　　）内の音は呑み込むように、⌣の部分はリンキングして、/ の部分ではポーズを置いて発音します。

1. Companies will **now** be re**quire(d)** to cre**ate**⌣an⌣**a(t)**mos**phere** / that⌣en**cour**ages⌣em**ploy**ees / to **ta(ke)** the **leave**.

> ⤷POINT atmosphere の t で舌先を歯茎に付けたら、離さずそのまま m に移る。

2. Despi**(te)** the **gov**ernment's⌣**ef**forts, / **man**y **men**⌣are **still** re**luc**tan(t) to **ta(ke)** the **time**⌣**off**.

> ⤷POINT men の語末の n は次の are に必ずリンキングさせる。

3. The **com**pany al**lows work**ers / to par**ti**ci**pate**⌣in⌣**online meet**ings with their **chil**dren / at **home**.

> ⤷POINT allow は「アロウ」ではないので注意。

Defining

DL 047 CD2-30

1. ①〜⑧の定義に当てはまる語を本文から選んで書き、音声で確認しましょう。

2. 次のペアワークをしましょう。終わったら、役割を交代しましょう。

Aさん＝教科書を見ながらランダムに①〜⑧の定義を言う
Bさん＝何も見ずにAさんの定義に該当する単語を答える

① (p _ _ _ _ _ _ _ _) = the state of being someone's father

② (l _ _ _ _) = time when one has permission to be absent from work

③ (o _ _ _ _ _) = to make something legally or morally necessary

④ (r _ _ _ _ _ _ _ _) = slow, unwilling, and hesitant

⑤ (s _ _ _ _ _ _ _ _ _) = someone who watches over and directs another person

⑥ (c _ _ _ _ _ _ _ _) = a person one works with in a profession

⑦ (d _ _ _ _ _ _ _ _) = showing a hopeless sense that a situation is too bad to deal with

⑧ (e _ _ _ _ _) = to be greater in number or size than

Repeating

DL 048 CD2-31

1. ①〜⑧の空欄を **Defining** の正解の語あるいはその変化形・派生語で埋め、音声で確認しましょう。**Defining** のそれぞれの語は一度しか使えません。

2. 次のペアワークをしましょう。終わったら、役割を交代しましょう。

Aさん＝教科書を見ながらランダムに①〜⑧を1文ずつ音読する
Bさん＝何も見ずにそれを繰り返す
Aさん＝（　　）の箇所を「ピー」に代えて、①〜⑧の文をランダムに音読する
Bさん＝（　　）内の単語を答える

① She asked for a (　　　　　　　　　　　　) of absence to attend a funeral.

② Heavy fines are imposed on drivers who (　　　　　　　　　　) the speed limit.

③ To confirm the (　　　　　　　　　　) of the child, a DNA test is required.

④ His (　　　　　　　　　) to answer my questions made me suspicious.

⑤ I don't discuss private matters with my (　　　　　　　　　).

⑥ We have a moral (　　　　　　　　　　) to protect the environment.

⑦ Proper (　　　　　　　　) is essential when children are swimming.

⑧ Rescue teams worked (　　　　　　　　　　) to save those trapped underneath the collapsed building.

Retelling
 DL 049 · CD2-32

次のキーワードを利用しながら本文の要約を言ってみましょう。例は音声で確認できます。

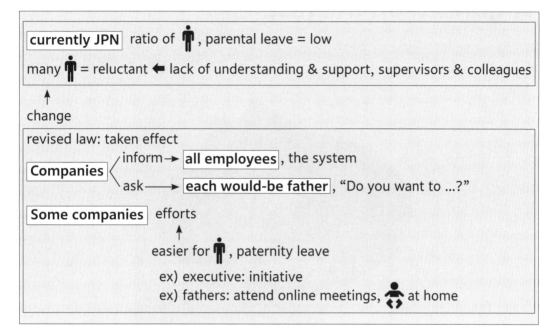

Commenting
 DL 050 · CD2-33

1〜10は本文の内容に関連するコメントです。自分の考えに似たコメントがあれば組み合わせたり、意見を付け加えたりして、自分の考えとしてパートナーに伝えてみましょう。

1. When I become a father, I will definitely take parental leave.
2. When I become a mother, I want my partner to take parental leave.
3. I still believe that the primary carer of a child should be the mother, not the father.
4. Men and women should be equally responsible for bringing up their own children.
5. We need to reform working patterns so that men can take parental leave without worrying.
6. It is necessary to create an environment where people can take any kind of leave they need without worrying.
7. It should be compulsory to take parental leave regardless of gender.
8. The revised law is not thorough enough. There should be incentives to take parental leave.
9. I suspect that some men don't want to take parental leave because they don't want to take care of the child.
10. It is good that the senior management of a company takes the initiative to take parental leave.

Unit 8

Veganism on the Rise

野菜から作った「豚骨ラーメン」

Chikaranomoto Holdings Co., Ltd.

Reading

○ CD2-34 ～ ○ CD2-46

1　　　Vegans in Japan are finding life much easier with a wide variety of foods
2　to choose from, including specialty items such as "pork bone" ramen and even
3　"cheesecake." Behind the trend are a growing health awareness among people who
4　want to avoid high-fat foods and advances in veganism technology in producing
5　meat alternatives.

6　　　"There isn't a food that can't be reproduced," said an official from the Japan
7　Vegan Society. In the strictest sense, a vegan does not eat any foods derived from
8　animals, such as meat, eggs, dairy products or even honey. Vegans also typically
9　avoid the use of animal products.

10　　　At its outlet in the Lumine Est Shinjuku shopping center in Tokyo, Ippudo,
11　a nationwide Hakata ramen chain, offers a plant-based *tonkotsu* (pork bone)
12　flavor ramen. The broth of the conventional noodle dish, originally from Fukuoka
13　Prefecture, has a pork-bone base.

14　　　The ramen served exclusively at the Ippudo restaurant in Shinjuku looks and
15　smells like the real thing but uses no ingredients derived from animals. Instead,
16　the broth is made from soybean milk mixed with a special oil, while the *chāshū*

braised pork combines soybean meat, lotus root and other ingredients. 17

The shop's *tonkotsu* flavor ramen "is not only free of animal meat but also 18 delivers taste" and is "popular with people irrespective of age and gender," 19 said Hidenobu Tomita, in charge at Chikaranomoto Group, which operates the 20 nationwide ramen restaurant chain. 21

Upbeet! Tokyo produces gluten-free donuts, cheesecakes and other sweets 22 using no eggs or butter. Vegan food is attractive because "people of different values 23 can enjoy it together," said the company head Nozomi Jinguji. 24

In her previous occupation as an airline flight attendant, Jinguji experienced 25 a variety of dietary cultures around the world. With a desire to "convey the joy of 26 food," she quit her job in search of food that everyone can enjoy, regardless of their 27 religious and cultural backgrounds. She settled on vegan cuisine. 28

In 2018, she founded Upbeet! Tokyo, which now supplies vegan sweets to 29 department stores, supermarkets, convenience stores and other retailers. The 30 company uses fermented soybeans as an alternative to cheese for its cheesecake, 31 which is in popular demand. 32

While some vegans do not eat meat for religious reasons, veganism is becoming 33 popular as a part of people's diets in some countries. 34

The selection of Tokyo in 2013 to host the 2020 Summer Olympics and 35 Paralympics and the anticipation of visitors from abroad with various dietary 36 practices is one reason veganism spread in Japan. 37

Many people who eat meat have partially adopted veganism in their diet, 38 enjoying it in a relaxed way. They also hope to avoid lifestyle-related diseases and 39 are concerned that increasing meat consumption contributes to global warming. 40

Likewise, the practice is getting a boost from advances in plant-based food 41 technology. For example, it is already possible to produce meat alternatives from 42 soybeans or wheat, among other ingredients, and butter substitutes from soy milk 43 or coconut oil. 44

According to Mayumi Muroya, a model and actress who heads the Tokyo-based 45 Japan Vegan Society, "Vegan meals are good for your health and the environment. 46 I recommend people have fun and try them." 47

Kyodo / The Japan Times

(519 words)

 Notes

ℓ.17　braise「とろ火で蒸煮する」　　ℓ.28　settle on ~「(いろいろあった後)~に決める、~に落ち着く」

1. ①〜㉕の日本語に相当する表現のかたまりを本文から抜き出し、音声で確認しましょう。

（　　）内の数字は語数を表し、数字の後に「／分」とあれば、該当部分が本文中で連続していないことを表します。

2. 次のペアワークをしましょう。終わったら、役割を交代しましょう。

Aさん＝教科書を見ながらランダムに①〜㉕の日本語を言う

Bさん＝何も見ずにAさんの日本語に該当する英語を答える

① 食品の多様な選択肢（8）	
② 高まる健康意識（4）	
③ 高脂質食品を避けたい人々（7）	
④ 再現できない食べ物（6）	
⑤ 最も厳密な意味では（4）	
⑥ 乳製品（2）	
⑦ その伝統的麺料理（＝ラーメン）のスープ（7）	
⑧ 見た目も匂いも本物のようだ（7）	
⑨ 動物に由来する具材（4）	
⑩ れんこん（2）	
⑪ 動物の肉が入っていない（4）	
⑫ 年齢や性別に関係なく（5）	
⑬ 価値観が異なる人々（4）	
⑭ 彼女の前職で（4）	
⑮ 食の喜びを伝える（5）	
⑯ 誰もが楽しめる食べ物を探して（8）	
⑰ 宗教的、文化的背景にかかわらず（7）	
⑱ 発酵大豆（2）	
⑲ チーズ代替品として（5）	
⑳ 海外からの訪問客（3）	
㉑ 多様な食習慣を持った（4）	
㉒ 生活習慣病を避ける（3）	
㉓ 地球温暖化につながる（4）	
㉔ 大豆か小麦から肉代替品を作り出す（7）	
㉕ 豆乳かココナツオイルからバター代替品を作り出す（9／分）	

Choosing

 DL 052   CD2-48

1. ①〜⑤の [   ] 内のどちらの語を選ぶと true になるか考え、音声で確認しましょう。

2. 次のペアワークをしましょう。終わったら、役割を交代しましょう。

> Aさん＝ [   ] 内のどちらかの語を選び、①〜⑤の文全体をランダムに音読する
> Bさん＝何も見ずにAさんの音読を聞き、それが true か false かを判定する。
> さらに、true ならそのまま繰り返し、false なら訂正する。

① The reason vegans in Japan are finding life easier [is / is not] because non-vegans have become vegans.

② The technology has advanced to produce plant-based foods that not only look like animal-based foods but also taste like [animal-based / plant-based] foods.

③ Traditional *tonkotsu* ramen is a noodle dish with broth made from [pork bones / soy beans].

④ Jinguji's wish [is / is not] that everyone should be vegan, regardless of religion or culture.

⑤ The argument that eating animal meat is not ethical from an animal welfare point of view [is / is not] addressed in this article.

Oral Reading

 DL 053   CD2-49

音声イメージが可視化された文を見ながら音声を聞き、まねて音読しましょう。

太い部分は長めに、それ以外は短めに、(   ) 内の音は呑み込むように、‿の部分はリンキングして、/ の部分ではポーズを置いて発音します。

1. Vegans‿in Ja**pan** / are **find**ing **life much‿eas**ier / with‿a **wi(de)** va**ri**ety of **foods** to **choose** from.

> POINT   easier の si 部分は「ジ」でなく「ズィ」/zi/。

2. Be**hin(d)** the **trend** / are a(d)**vanc**es‿in **veg**anism te(ch)**nol**ogy / in pro**duc**ing **meat‿**al**ter**natives.

> POINT   advances の d を「ド」、technology の ch を「ク」と言わない（母音を付けない）。

3. They are con**cerned** / that‿in**creas**ing **mea(t)** con**sump**tion / con**trib**utes to **glob**al **warm**ing.

> POINT   contributes は第2音節が強い。

Defining

🎧 DL 054　◉ CD2-50

1. ①〜⑧の定義に当てはまる語を本文から選んで書き、音声で確認しましょう。

2. 次のペアワークをしましょう。終わったら、役割を交代しましょう。

> Aさん＝教科書を見ながらランダムに①〜⑧の定義を言う
> Bさん＝何も見ずにAさんの定義に該当する単語を答える

① (a _ _ _ _ _ _ _ _ _ _) = something one can choose instead of something else

② (o _ _ _ _ _) = a place from which goods are sold or distributed

③ (i _ _ _ _ _ _ _ _ _) = any of the foods that are combined to make a particular dish

④ (c _ _ _ _ _ _) = a style or method of cooking

⑤ (r _ _ _ _ _ _ _) = a business that sells goods directly to the public

⑥ (a _ _ _ _ _ _ _ _ _ _ _) = the act of expecting or predicting something

⑦ (c _ _ _ _ _ _ _ _ _ _) = the eating or drinking of something

⑧ (b _ _ _ _) = something that helps something increase or improve

Repeating

🎧 DL 055　◉ CD2-51

1. ①〜⑧の空欄を Defining の正解の語あるいはその変化形・派生語で埋め、音声で確認しましょう。Defining のそれぞれの語は一度しか使えません。

2. 次のペアワークをしましょう。終わったら、役割を交代しましょう。

> Aさん＝教科書を見ながらランダムに①〜⑧を1文ずつ音読する
> Bさん＝何も見ずにそれを繰り返す
> Aさん＝（　　）の箇所を「ピー」に代えて、①〜⑧の文をランダムに音読する
> Bさん＝（　　）内の単語を答える

① There is growing (　　　　　　　　　　) that the prime minister will have to resign.

② Winning this award was a real (　　　　　　　　　　) to his ego.

③ Coconut is a basic (　　　　　　　　) for many curries.

④ You can relax on the beach or, (　　　　　　　　　　), try visiting the bustling town center.

⑤ Japanese (　　　　　　　　) is known for being low in fat.

⑥ They have retail (　　　　　　　　) in every major European city.

⑦ This food is not fit for human (　　　　　　　　).

⑧ We are looking for someone with (　　　　　　　　) experience.

Retelling  DL 056　CD2-52

次のキーワードを利用しながら本文の要約を言ってみましょう。例は音声で確認できます。

| **Vegans** | = NOT eat <u>foods from animals</u>

　　　　　　　　　 ex) meat, eggs, dairy products, honey
<past> vegans, JPN: difficult, find things to eat
<now> changing
　　⇨ variety ↗

2 factors contributing to trend
(1) health consciousness of people ↗
　 × high-fat foods

(2) vegan technology ↗
　 meat alternatives
　　　 ex) Ippudo: ramen ⟵————— pork-bone flavor but plant-based
　　　　　 Upbeet! Tokyo: sweets ⟵ w/o eggs or butter

　　　　　　　　　　　　　　　　　　 ↗ people's health
| **Japan Vegan Society** | vegan meals are good ⟨
　　　　　　　　　　　　　　　　　　 ↘ environ.

Commenting  DL 057　CD2-53

1～10は本文の内容に関連するコメントです。自分の考えに似たコメントがあれば組み合わせたり、意見を付け加えたりして、自分の考えとしてパートナーに伝えてみましょう。

1. I would like to try plant-based *tonkotsu* ramen.

2. I would like to try plant-based sweets.

3. I have tried vegan food such as soya meat for health reasons.

4. I love beef and don't want to think about cows being killed for it.

5. I think that from now on people should basically eat plant-based food. It will be better for the environment.

6. It is good that people can casually enjoy vegan food whenever they want, regardless of their principles.

7. Killing animals and killing plants are basically the same thing. That is why I don't understand veganism.

8. Whether I eat vegan food or not depends on whether it tastes good.

9. I want to go vegan for the sake of the environment.

10. I am not sure that a vegan diet gives me a balanced diet.

Same-Sex Partnership Oath System

東京都パートナーシップ宣誓制度

Reading

CD2-54 ~ CD2-67

1　　Tokyo's same-sex partnership system came into effect Tuesday, allowing sexual
2　minority couples in the capital to be treated in the same manner as married
3　heterosexual couples in areas such as housing, health care and child-rearing.

4　　However, same-sex marriage is prohibited nationwide, meaning various other
5　legal protections only afforded to heterosexual married couples remain unavailable.

6　　Still, the Tokyo Partnership Oath System, despite its limitations, has been
7　celebrated by many in the LGBTQ community as a step toward achieving equal
8　rights for sexual minorities in Japan.

9　　"As a 41-year-old sexual minority and Tokyo resident, it's a joy to have my
10　presence finally acknowledged practically for the first time," said Fumino Sugiyama,
11　a transgender activist and vice representative of Partnership Act for Tokyo.

12　　Activist Soyoka Yamamoto, a representative of the same group, said the new
13　system, though not legally binding, does substantially address many of the concerns
14　Tokyo same-sex couples had and entitles them to various city services.

15　　"But we cannot pause here," Yamamoto said, adding that the partnership
16　system can serve as a catalyst for achieving a society where the rights of sexual

minorities in Japan are equally protected.   17

Tokyo is the ninth prefecture to fully implement a partnership system since   18
the capital's Shibuya and Setagaya wards introduced their own in 2015. Over 200   19
municipalities currently have such a system, and its introduction in Tokyo means   20
that more than 60% of the Japanese population is now similarly covered.   21

Couples with at least one person who identifies as a sexual minority can now   22
apply for official recognition of their partnership if one half of the partnership   23
lives, studies or works in Tokyo or plans to move to the prefecture within the next   24
three months.   25

Guidelines produced by the human rights division of the Tokyo Metropolitan   26
Government state that the system has been introduced in order to "create an   27
environment where sexual minorities can live comfortably," by, for example,   28
removing administrative barriers in daily life.   29

This will serve to deepen the general understanding of gender diversity and   30
create a society in which "everyone can play an active role in their own way," the   31
guidelines say.   32

Upon registering for the partnership system, couples are issued a "certificate   33
of acceptance" that can then be used as proof of their partnership when accessing   34
previously unavailable public and private services.   35

Under the system, people can use public family housing services, give consent   36
for surgery, be considered a family when applying for housing loans and insurance,   37
and have the right to make hospital visits. Applicants with children may also   38
include each child's name on their certificate.   39

However, the partnership system remains separate from the marriage system,   40
which is a legal act defined in the Civil Code. As the legally non-binding system   41
requires no changes to the family registry, certain key rights granted to married   42
heterosexual couples—such as inheritance, joint custody of children and spousal   43
tax deductions—remain denied.   44

Despite polls suggesting that the public is generally in favor of legalizing   45
same-sex marriage, Japan is the only country in the Group of Seven yet to take   46
steps to do so.   47

The Japan Times

(511 words)

 Notes

ℓ.1   come into effect「発効する、施行される」

ℓ.46   the Group of Seven「先進 7 カ国（略称G7。フランス、アメリカ、イギリス、ドイツ、日本、イタ
リア、カナダ（議長国順）の 7 カ国と欧州連合（EU）が参加するグループ）」

Chunking

DL 058 · CD2-68

1. ①～㉕の日本語に相当する表現のかたまりを本文から抜き出し、音声で確認しましょう。

（　　）内の数字は語数を表し、数字の後に「／分」とあれば、該当部分が本文中で連続していないことを表します。

2. 次のペアワークをしましょう。終わったら、役割を交代しましょう。

Aさん＝教科書を見ながらランダムに①～㉕の日本語を言う

Bさん＝何も見ずにAさんの日本語に該当する英語を答える

① 同様に扱われる（6）	
② 既婚の異性愛カップル（3）	
③ 住まい、医療、子育て（5）	
④ さまざまな他の法的保護（4）	
⑤ 利用できないままである（2）	
⑥ その限界にかかわらず（3）	
⑦ 自分の存在を認知してもらう（4／分）	
⑧ 法的拘束力はないが（4）	
⑨ 同性カップルが抱いていた不安（5／分）	
⑩ きっかけとなる（4）	
⑪ パートナーシップ制度を完全実施する（5）	
⑫ 少なくとも片方が性的マイノリティと自認するカップル（12）	
⑬ 自分たちのパートナーシップの公的認知を申請する（7）	
⑭ 東京都の人権部（9）	
⑮ 行政的障壁を取り除くこと（3）	
⑯ 性の多様性についての一般的な理解（6）	
⑰ 活躍できる（5）	
⑱ 受理証明書（4）	
⑲ 以前は利用できなかった公的・私的サービス（6）	
⑳ 公営住宅サービス（4）	
㉑ 手術に同意する（4）	
㉒ 住宅ローンや保険に申し込むとき（7）	
㉓ 民法で定義された法的行為（8）	
㉔ 子どもの共同親権（4）	
㉕ 配偶者控除（3）	

Choosing

 DL 059 CD2-69

1. ①〜⑤の [   ] 内のどちらの語を選ぶと true になるか考え、音声で確認しましょう。

2. 次のペアワークをしましょう。終わったら、役割を交代しましょう。

> Aさん＝ [   ] 内のどちらかの語を選び、①〜⑤の文全体をランダムに音読する
> Bさん＝何も見ずにAさんの音読を聞き、それが true か false かを判定する。
> さらに、true ならそのまま繰り返し、false なら訂正する。

① The new system allowed same-sex couples in Tokyo to [enjoy some new benefits / give up some old privileges].

② The introduction of the new system [does / does not] ensure that same-sex couples are treated in the same way as heterosexual married couples.

③ The introduction of the new system has generally been [welcomed / denounced] by the couples concerned.

④ Under the new system, on the death of one person in a same-sex couple, the partner [can / cannot] inherit the deceased's property.

⑤ Same-sex marriage is currently [legal / illegal] in the US, UK, France, Germany, Canada and Italy.

Oral Reading

 DL 060 CD2-70

音声イメージが可視化された文を見ながら音声を聞き、まねて音読しましょう。
太い部分は長めに、それ以外は短めに、（   ）内の音は呑み込むように、⌣の部分はリンキングして、/ の部分ではポーズを置いて発音します。

1. The **To**ky**o Par(t)**ner**ship**⌣**Oath Sys**tem / has been **celebrat**e(d) by **man**y in the **LGBTQ** com**mu**nity.

> POINT community の mu は「ミュー」と伸ばす。

2. The **new sys**tem sub**stan**tially ad**dress**es / **man**y of the con**cerns To**ky**o same**-**sex cou**ples **had**.

> POINT system の sy は「シ」ではなく「スィ」/si/。

3. Ja**pan**⌣is the **on**ly **coun**try in the **Group**⌣of **Sev**en / **ye(t)** to **take steps** to **le**gal**ize same**-**sex mar**riage.

> POINT marriage の語末の音 /dʒ/ は、ほとんど無声でよい。

Defining

1. ①～⑧の定義に当てはまる語を本文から選んで書き、音声で確認しましょう。

2. 次のペアワークをしましょう。終わったら、役割を交代しましょう。

> Aさん＝教科書を見ながらランダムに①～⑧の定義を言う
> Bさん＝何も見ずにAさんの定義に該当する単語を答える

① (p _ _ _ _ _ _ _) = to formally forbid by law or rule

② (r _ _ _ _ _ _ _ _ _ _ _ _) = someone chosen to act or speak for someone else

③ (s _ _ _ _ _ _ _ _ _ _ _) = to a great and significant extent

④ (a _ _ _ _ _ _) = to think about and begin to deal with

⑤ (d _ _ _ _ _ _ _ _) = the state of showing a great deal of variety

⑥ (c _ _ _ _ _ _) = permission for something to happen

⑦ (i _ _ _ _ _ _ _ _) = an arrangement in which a company guarantees compensation for specified loss or damage in return for specified payment

⑧ (d _ _ _ _ _ _ _) = the act of taking away an amount from a total

Repeating

DL 062　CD2-72

1. ①～⑧の空欄を **Defining** の正解の語あるいはその変化形・派生語で埋め、音声で確認しましょう。**Defining** のそれぞれの語は一度しか使えません。

2. 次のペアワークをしましょう。終わったら、役割を交代しましょう。

> Aさん＝教科書を見ながらランダムに①～⑧を1文ずつ音読する
> Bさん＝何も見ずにそれを繰り返す
> Aさん＝（　　）の箇所を「ピー」に代えて、①～⑧の文をランダムに音読する
> Bさん＝（　　）内の単語を答える

① Foreigners may be surprised to learn that drinking in public is not ( ) in Japan.

② In my view, the committee deliberately failed to ( ) the core issue.

③ They can't publish your name without your ( ).

④ He was the Queen's ( ) at the ceremony.

⑤ New York is a very culturally and ethnically ( ) city.

⑥ How much will it cost to ( ) my car against accidents?

⑦ The deer population has increased ( ) in recent years.

⑧ No ( ) in pay is made for absence due to illness.

Retelling 🎧 DL 063 💿 CD2-73

次のキーワードを利用しながら本文の要約を言ってみましょう。例は音声で確認できます。

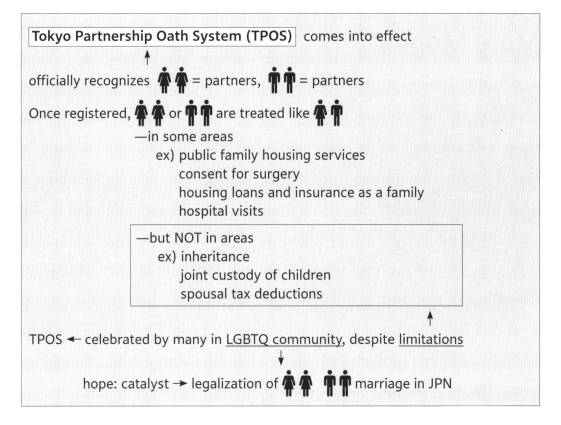

Commenting 🎧 DL 064 💿 CD2-74

1～10は本文の内容に関連するコメントです。自分の考えに似たコメントがあれば組み合わせたり、意見を付け加えたりして、自分の考えとしてパートナーに伝えてみましょう。

1. Japan should legalize same-sex marriage. It would not harm anyone.
2. Personally, I am not comfortable with allowing same-sex marriage. In fact, about one third of the countries in the UN stipulate sexual acts between same sex people as illegal.
3. I feel that the public's perception of same-sex marriage has changed recently.
4. The partnership system is not enough, but I welcome it as a first step.
5. It makes me sad to think that there are still municipalities that don't even have a partnership system.
6. I was surprised that Tokyo wasn't the first city to introduce the system.
7. This system alone is not enough for sexual minorities to live comfortably.
8. The laws should be changed to allow more diverse family arrangements.
9. We should look at the status of same-sex marriages around the world.
10. I will take part in activities such as signing petitions to have same-sex marriages legalized.

Unit 10

Get Out of Japan to Earn More Money?!

外国に「出稼ぎ」に行く若者たち

Reading ⊙ CD2-75 ~ ⊙ CD2-86

1   Some young Japanese workers have found that with a little boldness and hard
2 work there are opportunities to be had and money to be made beyond the nation's
3 borders.

4   Shizuoka native Toshiya Hayama (a pseudonym) recently saved a significant
5 amount of money as a participant on the Working Holiday program over the course
6 of two years in Australia, where the national minimum wage of $21.38 (¥1,990) per
7 hour is more than double the ¥961 available in Japan.

8   Combining his morning job as a hotel receptionist with night shifts as a food
9 delivery driver, he also cleaned the hostel where he was staying in exchange for
10 room and board, eventually saving $25,000 (¥2.35 million) over the course of ten
11 months.

12   Hayama has joined a growing number of people departing Japan, with the
13 number of Japanese migrants staying in other countries rising from 587,000 in
14 1989 to a peak three decades later of 1,410,000 in 2019.

15   Research conducted by University of Melbourne migration expert Nana Oishi
16 found that Japan's future economic prospects are a significant factor for many

choosing to emigrate. ~~17~~

Many of her Japanese interview subjects are highly skilled young and ~~18~~
mid-career workers who arrive on temporary visas or as working holiday makers ~~19~~
in search of a lifestyle change—particularly a better work-life balance than was ~~20~~
available to them in Japan. ~~21~~

Realizing that the available wages are also much higher, some of them begin ~~22~~
wanting to settle down in Australia, and start studying to get the right qualifications ~~23~~
to apply for longer-term skilled visas. ~~24~~

"As wages there are so high, it's now a popular place for people to go in order ~~25~~
to work, earn money and then come back home with what they have saved," said ~~26~~
Japan Association for Working Holiday Makers public relations staffer Kotaro ~~27~~
Sanada. "With the depreciation of the yen, the initial investment is expensive, but ~~28~~
you can make a lot of money while you're there," he added. ~~29~~

For 23-year-old working holiday maker Daisuke Nakajima (a pseudonym), who ~~30~~
himself recently departed Japan for Australia, the decision was simple. "Right now, ~~31~~
if you work a normal job in Japan, you can expect to take home maybe ¥150,000 ~~32~~
to ¥200,000 per month on average, but if you do the same job overseas, you could ~~33~~
make anything from ¥300,000 to ¥800,000 per month," he said. ~~34~~

"Working in Japan just doesn't make any sense," he said, explaining that he ~~35~~
planned to remain overseas earning money in foreign currency until he turns ~~36~~
30, at which point he will use what he has saved to return home and invest in ~~37~~
Japanese real estate. ~~38~~

But the situation may not be quite as simple as that, said Yuki Hashimoto, an ~~39~~
economist at the Research Institute of Economy, Trade and Industry. Workers, she ~~40~~
said, may find that an extended period overseas diminishes their career prospects ~~41~~
at home, should they ever wish to return to work in Japan. "Large companies in ~~42~~
particular only tend to hire recent university graduates," she added. ~~43~~

On the other hand, for those leavers who decide to stay overseas long term or ~~44~~
even forever, she said, "I really don't think there are any disadvantages." ~~45~~

The Japan Times

(520 words)

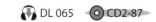
1. ①〜㉕の日本語に相当する表現のかたまりを本文から抜き出し、音声で確認しましょう。
（　　）内の数字は語数を表し、数字の後に「／分」とあれば、該当部分が本文中で連続していないことを表します。

2. 次のペアワークをしましょう。終わったら、役割を交代しましょう。

　　Ａさん＝教科書を見ながらランダムに①〜㉕の日本語を言う
　　Ｂさん＝何も見ずにＡさんの日本語に該当する英語を答える

① 少しの大胆さと頑張りがあれば（7）	
② 日本の国境を越えたところに（4）	
③ かなりの額のお金を貯めた（6）	
④ 2年の間に（6）	
⑤ 国で決められた最低賃金（4）	
⑥ ホテルの受付としての朝の仕事（6）	
⑦ 食材配送ドライバーとしての夜勤（7）	
⑧ 部屋代と食事代をただにしてもらう代わりに（6）	
⑨ 日本を出ていく人々（3）	
⑩ メルボルン大学の移住研究の専門家（5）	
⑪ 将来の経済的見通し（3）	
⑫ 移住を選択する多くの人たち（4）	
⑬ インタビューを受けた日本人協力者（3）	
⑭ 高い技能をもった若い労働者（4／分）	
⑮ 高い技能をもった中堅労働者（4／分）	
⑯ 短期滞在ビザでやってくる（4）	
⑰ ワーキングホリデーのためにやってくる（5／分）	
⑱ 生活様式の変化を求めて（6）	
⑲ オーストラリアに落ち着く（4）	
⑳ 適切な資格を取る（4）	
㉑ より長期の技能ビザを申請する（5）	
㉒ 広報担当スタッフ（3）	
㉓ 円の下落（5）	
㉔ 初期投資（3）	
㉕ 外貨で稼ぎながら（5）	

Choosing  DL 066　CD2-88

1. ①〜⑤の [　　] 内のどちらの語を選ぶと true になるか考え、音声で確認しましょう。

2. 次のペアワークをしましょう。終わったら、役割を交代しましょう。

Aさん＝ [　　] 内のどちらかの語を選び、①〜⑤の文全体をランダムに音読する

Bさん＝何も見ずにAさんの音読を聞き、それが true か false かを判定する。
さらに、true ならそのまま繰り返し、false なら訂正する。

① Some young Japanese have found that there are ways to make more money [inside / outside] Japan.

② Hayama left Japan and has made [significantly / marginally] more money than he could have in his home country.

③ It is indicated that an important reason why Japanese people emigrate is because they are [optimistic / pessimistic] about Japan's future economy.

④ Many of Oishi's survey respondents came to Australia with the intention of [staying temporarily / settling down].

⑤ Hashimoto suggests that staying overseas too long [will / will not] make it difficult to return to work in Japan.

Oral Reading  DL 067　CD2-89

音声イメージが可視化された文を見ながら音声を聞き、まねて音読しましょう。

太い部分は長めに、それ以外は短めに、(　　) 内の音は呑み込むように、⌣の部分はリンキングして、/ の部分ではポーズを置いて発音します。

1. Ja**pan's fu**ture eco**nom**ic **pros**pects / are a si(g)**ni**ficant **fa(c)**tor / for **man**y **choos**ing to emi**grate**.

POINT choos<u>ing</u>の下線部は「ジ」でなく「ズィ」/zi/。

2. **Re**al**iz**ing tha(t) the a**vail**able **wag**es⌣are **al**so **much high**er, / **some** be**gin want**ing to **set**tle **down**⌣in⌣Aus**tral**ia.

POINT realizing は舌先をどこにも付けない R 音で始まり、舌先を歯茎に付ける L 音に移る。

3. **Work**ers may **fin(d)** / that⌣an⌣ex**tend**e(d) **pe**riod⌣**o**ver**seas** di**min**ishes their ca**reer pros**pects⌣at **home**.

POINT that 節は、ポーズを置くなら that の後ろでなく前に。

efining

1. ①〜⑧の定義に当てはまる語を本文から選んで書き、音声で確認しましょう。

2. 次のペアワークをしましょう。終わったら、役割を交代しましょう。

> Aさん＝教科書を見ながらランダムに①〜⑧の定義を言う
> Bさん＝何も見ずにAさんの定義に該当する単語を答える

① (w _ _ _) = a fixed regular payment made by an employer to an employee, especially to a manual or unskilled worker

② (b _ _ _ _) = the provision of regular meals when one stays somewhere

③ (p _ _ _ _ _ _ _) = the possibility of some future event or situation occurring

④ (s _ _ _ _ _ _) = a person who is the focus of a study or experiment

⑤ (q _ _ _ _ _ _ _ _ _ _ _ _) = a quality that makes someone suitable for a particular job

⑥ (d _ _ _ _ _ _ _ _ _ _ _) = a reduction in the value of something

⑦ (i _ _ _ _ _) = to spend money with the expectation of achieving profit

⑧ (d _ _ _ _ _ _ _) = make or become less

Repeating

1. ①〜⑧の空欄を **Defining** の正解の語あるいはその変化形・派生語で埋め、音声で確認しましょう。**Defining** のそれぞれの語は一度しか使えません。

2. 次のペアワークをしましょう。終わったら、役割を交代しましょう。

> Aさん＝教科書を見ながらランダムに①〜⑧を1文ずつ音読する
> Bさん＝何も見ずにそれを繰り返す
>
> Aさん＝（　　）の箇所を「ピー」に代えて、①〜⑧の文をランダムに音読する
> Bさん＝（　　）内の単語を答える

① We're having difficulty recruiting enough (　　　　　　　　　) staff.

② The (　　　　　　　　) of the study were randomly selected from a local university.

③ There is an element of risk in any (　　　　　　　　).

④ Is there any (　　　　　　　　) of the weather improving?

⑤ A (　　　　　　　) increase of 5% is demanded by the union.

⑥ If you book full (　　　　　　　　), you will receive breakfast, lunch and dinner.

⑦ New cars (　　　　　　　　) quickly in the first two years.

⑧ We should try to (　　　　　　　) the cost of production.

Retelling 🎧 DL 070　◎ CD2-92

次のキーワードを利用しながら本文の要約を言ってみましょう。例は音声で確認できます。

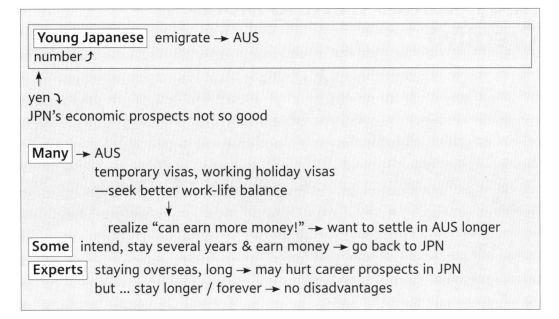

Young Japanese emigrate → AUS
number ↗

↑
yen ↘
JPN's economic prospects not so good

Many → AUS
　　　temporary visas, working holiday visas
　　　—seek better work-life balance
　　　　　　　↓
　　　realize "can earn more money!" → want to settle in AUS longer
Some intend, stay several years & earn money → go back to JPN
Experts staying overseas, long → may hurt career prospects in JPN
　　　but ... stay longer / forever → no disadvantages

Commenting 🎧 DL 071　◎ CD2-93

1〜10は本文の内容に関連するコメントです。自分の考えに似たコメントがあれば組み合わせたり、意見を付け加えたりして、自分の考えとしてパートナーに伝えてみましょう。

1. I want to work in Australia to earn more money.

2. I want to work abroad to learn English and experience the local culture.

3. I don't want to work abroad because there are many unsafe places.

4. In the future, I would like to live abroad for the rest of my life.

5. Exchange rates change, so I want to find the right time to work abroad.

6. We should think more seriously about why wages and salaries are not rising in Japan.

7. I don't think it will be easy to find a good job in Japan after working abroad for a long time.

8. I am sure that the experience of working abroad will be useful when I come back to live in Japan.

9. Working abroad is not all good, with problems such as non-payment of wages and various kinds of harassment.

10. Many foreigners work in Japan, for example in convenience stores, but I wonder if the wages are higher in Japan than in their home countries.

Baby Names Getting More Creative

キラキラネーム増加中、その理由とは

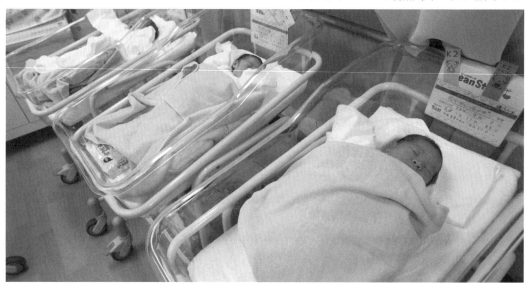

Jiji Press Photo

Reading

CD3-02 ~ CD3-09

1   Yuji Ogihara, a cultural psychologist at Tokyo University of Science, has
2 been studying naming patterns in Japan since 2015. In a 2022 study, he and his
3 colleague looked at a total of 58,485 baby names published in newsletters from 10
4 municipalities across Japan. Using data from 1979 to 2018, the team found that
5 the rate of names that appeared only once in their municipality increased over the
6 40-year period.

7   This was consistent with Ogihara's previous research. In a 2015 study,
8 instead of looking at unique baby names, Ogihara looked at the most common
9 ones. He found that over about 10 years, the rates of the 10 most popular name
10 pronunciations decreased, which he says implies a rise in unique ones.

11   What exactly makes a name unique or uncommon? There aren't that many
12 options for unusual written names since the Japanese government maintains a
13 list of approximately 3,000 characters that parents are required to pick from. As
14 a result, the greatest potential for unique names lies in the pronunciation, which
15 the government doesn't restrict.

16   The popular given name 大翔 is commonly pronounced "Hiroto," but it has

at least 18 other pronunciations, including "Yamato" and "Taiga." In his research, Ogihara also came across at least one 大翔 whose reading was "Tsubasa" and one "Sora." This next-level creativity can also be seen in one baby named 月, read Runa—that is, "luna," or another Latin-derived name for the moon. Ogihara also gives the example of a baby with the first name 光, with the reading Raito—"light."

There's another category of unique names, in which one character is left out of the pronunciation altogether. On paper, it enhances the meaning of the name, but it's dropped from the spoken version. A baby named 大空, meaning "expansive sky," is simply called "Sora" after the second kanji. One named 心結, which might mean something like "heart connection," is called "Kokoro," which leaves the second character unspoken.

This trend toward unique names shows that Japan is becoming more individualistic as a society, according to Ogihara. Generally speaking, babies assigned as male seem to be more likely to receive popular names than females. Ogihara says that it may be the fact that females are more likely to face pressure to conform that makes parents wish for their girls to stand out more. "Parents are trying to make their girls more independent and more unique compared to boys," Ogihara speculates.

In fact, research shows that names may be getting more unique in general, with similar results shown in China, the US, Germany and France. This makes sense. The world is getting more global and interconnected. As people are exposed to other cultures, they're exposed to more languages. Migration and movement, too, create more diversity and linguistic mixing.

Names are an elusive part of identity. Most of us are given them without having a say in the matter and are stuck with them without a chance to interrogate the reasoning. Perhaps that's why we find ourselves so eager to mine for meaning, in hopes they'll hold more clues to who we are.

The Japan Times

(507 words)

1. ①~㉕の日本語に相当する表現のかたまりを本文から抜き出し、音声で確認しましょう。
　（　　）内の数字は語数を表し、数字の後に「／分」とあれば、該当部分が本文中で連続していないことを表します。

2. 次のペアワークをしましょう。終わったら、役割を交代しましょう。

　　Aさん＝教科書を見ながらランダムに①~㉕の日本語を言う
　　Bさん＝何も見ずにAさんの日本語に該当する英語を答える

① その自治体で一度だけ現れた名前（8）	
② オギハラ氏の以前の研究と合致して（5）	
③ よくある名前の読みベスト10（6）	
④ 個性的な読みが増えたことを示唆する（6）	
⑤ 名前を個性的または珍しいものにする（6）	
⑥ 親がそこから選ばねばならない漢字の一覧表（11／分）	
⑦ ラテン語起源の月の呼び方（5）	
⑧ 読みから全く落とされて（6）	
⑨ その名前の意味を強める（6）	
⑩ 発音された名前からは落とされる（5）	
⑪ 「心のつながり」のような意味である（5）	
⑫ 二番目の漢字は読まない（5）	
⑬ 個性的な名前が増えつつあるこの傾向（5）	
⑭ 社会としてより個性的になってきている（7）	
⑮ 一般的に言って（2）	
⑯ 男性として生まれた赤ちゃん（4）	
⑰ よくある名前を授かる確率がより高い（6）	
⑱ 同調圧力にさらされる確率がより高い（7）	
⑲ 自分の娘がもっと目立ってほしいと願う（8）	
⑳ 自分の娘をより自立させ、より個性的にする（8）	
㉑ 辻褄が合う（2）	
㉒ グローバル化が進み相互のつながりが強まって（5）	
㉓ 多様性と多言語の混交を増進する（6）	
㉔ この件に関して自分の意見を言えずに（7）	
㉕ 自分たちが何者であるかを知る手がかり（5）	

Choosing    DL 073   CD3-11

1. ①～⑤の [   ] 内のどちらの語を選ぶと true になるか考え、音声で確認しましょう。

2. 次のペアワークをしましょう。終わったら、役割を交代しましょう。

> Aさん＝ [   ] 内のどちらかの語を選び、①～⑤の文全体をランダムに音読する
> Bさん＝何も見ずにAさんの音読を聞き、それが true か false かを判定する。
> さらに、true ならそのまま繰り返し、false なら訂正する。

① The 2022 study found a trend for Japanese names to become more [unique / traditional].

② The results of the 2015 and 2022 studies [support / contradict] each other.

③ Japanese names can be unique mainly by the way the characters are [combined / pronounced].

④ Ogihara speculates that female names are more unique because girls tend to be forced to be more [conventional / independent].

⑤ The phenomenon of names becoming more unique is observed [only / not only] in Japan.

Oral Reading    DL 074   CD3-12

音声イメージが可視化された文を見ながら音声を聞き、まねて音読しましょう。
太い部分は長めに、それ以外は短めに、(　　) 内の音は呑み込むように、‿の部分はリンキングして、/ の部分ではポーズを置いて発音します。

1. The **rate**‿of **names** / that‿ap**peared**‿**on**ly **once**‿in their mu**nic**i**pal**ity / in**creased**‿over the **for**ty-**year pe**riod.

> POINT   year の発音 /jɪər/ は、ear の発音 /ɪər/ とは違う。

2. The **great**es(t) po**ten**tial for u**ni(que) names** / **lies**‿in the pro**nun**ci**a**tion, / which the **gov**ernmen(t) **does**n'(t) re**strict**.

> POINT   ...tial と ...tion ははっきりと「シャル」「ション」と発音せず、あいまい母音を使う。

3. **Fe**males‿are **more like**ly to **face pres**sure to con**form**, / **so par**ents **wish** for their **girls** to **stand**‿**ou(t) more**.

> POINT   girls の ir 部分は暗い音色の母音を使う。

Defining

1. ①～⑧の定義に当てはまる語を本文から選んで書き、音声で確認しましょう。

2. 次のペアワークをしましょう。終わったら、役割を交代しましょう。

Aさん＝教科書を見ながら①～⑧の定義を言う

Bさん＝何も見ずにAさんの定義に該当する単語を答える

① (c _ _ _ _ _ _ _ _ _) = in agreement with something

② (r _ _ _ _ _ _ _) = to put a limit on; keep under control

③ (p _ _ _ _ _ _ _ _) = to produce the sound of (a word)

④ (e _ _ _ _ _ _) = to increase or improve the quality or value of

⑤ (c _ _ _ _ _ _) = to behave according to socially acceptable conventions or standards

⑥ (s _ _ _ _ _ _ _ _) = to form a theory about something without firm evidence

⑦ (e _ _ _ _ _ _) = difficult to find, catch, or achieve

⑧ (i _ _ _ _ _ _ _ _ _ _) = to ask formal questions of

Repeating

1. ①～⑧の空欄を **Defining** の正解の語あるいはその変化形・派生語で埋め、音声で確認しましょう。**Defining** のそれぞれの語は一度しか使えません。

2. 次のペアワークをしましょう。終わったら、役割を交代しましょう。

Aさん＝教科書を見ながらランダムに①～⑧を1文ずつ音読する

Bさん＝何も見ずにそれを繰り返す

Aさん＝ (　　) の箇所を「ピー」に代えて、①～⑧の文をランダムに音読する

Bさん＝ (　　) 内の単語を答える

① Japanese differs greatly from French in (　　　　　　　　　　　).

② He confessed after four days under (　　　　　　　　　).

③ Passing the English examination should (　　　　　　　　) your chances of getting the post.

④ We have to be (　　　　　　　　　　) in applying the rules.

⑤ A cure for the disease has proven to be (　　　　　　　　).

⑥ We (　　　　　　　　　) the number of students per class to 10.

⑦ The president's absence led to (　　　　　　　　　) over his health.

⑧ Students can be expelled for refusing to (　　　　　　　　) to school rules.

Retelling

次のキーワードを利用しながら本文の要約を言ってみましょう。例は音声で確認できます。

---

researcher studying name patters in JPN for yrs
  "unique names ↗, common names ↘"
    - % of names that appears once in each municipality ↗
    - % of the most common names ↘

Chinese characters: fixed ⟶ not unique
Pronunciation: NOT fixed ⟶ uniqueness

Unique names { pronunciation + pronunciation
                  漢字   漢字

interpretation: **JPN** becoming more individualistic, society
                names becoming more unique & diverse— **other countries as well**

Commenting

1〜10は本文の内容に関連するコメントです。自分の考えに似たコメントがあれば組み合わせたり、意見を付け加えたりして、自分の考えとしてパートナーに伝えてみましょう。

1. I know where my name comes from.

2. I think my name is relatively unique.

3. I think my name is relatively traditional.

4. I want to give my child a unique name.

5. I want to give my child a traditional name.

6. I will decide on my child's name, taking into consideration how it would sound abroad.

7. I don't understand parents who choose names that other people can't possibly read.

8. The government should not restrict the use of Chinese characters in names.

9. The government should not only restrict the use of Chinese characters but also the way they are read in names.

10. I don't think it is true that girls are expected to conform more than boys.

Japanese Love Affair With PET Bottles

PET ボトルの水平リサイクルを増やすために

Reading

CD3-17 ~ CD3-27

1   Japan has long had a love affair with the PET bottle. The clear, strong and
2 lightweight plastic outperformed aluminum, steel and glass to hold 76% of all
3 nonalcoholic drinks in the country in 2020, according to the Japan Soft Drinks
4 Association (JSDA).

5   Japan first adopted the material in 1977 for packaging soy sauce. In 1982, the
6 first heat-resistant PET bottle was developed. At first, liquids were limited to fruit
7 juice, closely followed by varieties of tea. Use for liquor was permitted in 1985.

8   Bottle size was restricted by the industry to 1 liter or more to curb waste,
9 but consumer demand for smaller containers and the introduction of PET bottle
10 recycling in the 1990s ushered in the release of 500-milliliter bottles in 1996.

11   As part of efforts to support the recycling process, beverage and PET bottle
12 manufacturing companies agreed that bottles were to be clear and made solely of
13 PET, with no direct printing on them.

14   However, the JSDA wants to do more. It is working toward 100% collection,
15 which would increase the recycling rate even further. One key way to achieve this
16 is by reducing contamination of bottles before collection.

Today, PET from homes is predominantly clean (rinsed, with cap and label removed). Large organizations also perform well, while buildings shared by numerous small and midsized enterprises tend to have less sorted recycling. Street collections fare worst. Contamination makes PET bottle recycling expensive and difficult at best and impossible at worst.

Collecting as much clean PET as possible is vital to promote "bottle-to-bottle" or "horizontal" recycling. This form of recycling can reduce or even avoid the use of virgin resin, a material derived from fossil fuels. The closed loop results in a 60% reduction in carbon dioxide compared to creating new PET from fossil-based resources.

At present, only 15.7% of PET bottles in Japan are produced by horizontal recycling. Most undergo downcycling, where their constituent materials are transformed into textiles or low-quality plastics. Although better than not recycling, once this process begins, recycling becomes harder and, ultimately, no longer possible. Recognizing these limitations, the JSDA declared in April 2021 that its members would achieve 50% bottle-to-bottle recycling by 2030.

One thing that the JSDA is trialing is a new kind of recycling box by vending machines. It features a lid difficult to open by consumers and a smaller, less visible opening to prevent it being used for trash. The box is orange—the same color as the branding for the United Nations' Sustainable Development Goal 11: Sustainable Cities and Communities—and labels convey key messages detailing the box's target waste.

Several large Japanese soft drink manufacturers are also appealing to consumers to dispose of PET bottles at work, in train stations and on the street as carefully as they do at home. In December 2020, Ito-en placed a "Tsubuseru Recycling Box" in Shibuya to raise awareness of its bottle-to-bottle efforts. The transparent bin was fitted with technology to compress each PET bottle in 20 seconds.

Although there is a "big journey" ahead, the JSDA is confident that the promise of "clean" PET will convince consumers to support the cause.

The Japan Times

(520 words)

Notes

ℓ.1   love affair 「熱狂、大好きであること」

ℓ.1   PET 「ポリエチレンテレフタレート (polyethylene terephthalate の略)」

ℓ.24   virgin resin 「未使用樹脂」

ℓ.24   closed loop 「閉じた輪 (製造工程で出る廃棄物を処理して再利用するシステム)」

ℓ.28   constituent 「成分である」

1. ①～㉙の日本語に相当する表現のかたまりを本文から抜き出し、音声で確認しましょう。

（　　）内の数字は語数を表し、数字の後に「／分」とあれば、該当部分が本文中で連続していないことを表します。

2. 次のペアワークをしましょう。終わったら、役割を交代しましょう。

　　Aさん＝教科書を見ながらランダムに①～㉙の日本語を言う
　　Bさん＝何も見ずにAさんの日本語に該当する英語を答える

① 透明で強く軽量の（4）	
② アルミ、スチール、ガラスを性能で上回った（5）	
③ 醤油を入れるのにその素材を採用した（7／分）	
④ 耐熱のPETボトル（3）	
⑤ 1リットル以上に制限されていた（7／分）	
⑥ 無駄を抑制するために（3）	
⑦ もっと小さな容器を求める消費者の声（5）	
⑧ 発売されるきっかけとなった（4）	
⑨ リサイクル支援の取り組みの一環として（9）	
⑩ 飲料そしてPETボトル製造業者（6）	
⑪ 透明でPETのみで作られていること（8）	
⑫ ボトルに直接印刷はせずに（6）	
⑬ リサイクル率をさらに高める（6）	
⑭ これを達成する一つの重要な方法（6）	
⑮ 収集前にボトルの汚れを減らすこと（6）	
⑯ 圧倒的にきれいである（3）	
⑰ キャップとラベルは取り除いてあり（5）	
⑱ 雑居ビル（8）	
⑲ 状況が最も悪い（2）	
⑳ PETボトルのリサイクルを良くて高価で困難なものにする（9）	
㉑ PETボトルのリサイクルを最悪だと不可能にする（7／分）	
㉒ 「水平」リサイクルを促進する（3／分）	
㉓ 化石燃料由来の原料（6）	
㉔ 二酸化炭素（排出）の減少（4）	
㉕ もはや不可能になる（4／分）	
㉖ こういう限界を認識し（3）	
㉗ 消費者が開けるのは難しいふた（7）	
㉘ それがゴミ箱にされるのを防ぐ（6）	
㉙ 消費者を説得しこの運動を支援させる（6）	

Choosing

 DL 080 · CD3-29

1. ①～⑤の [　　] 内のどちらの語を選ぶと true になるか考え、音声で確認しましょう。

2. 次のペアワークをしましょう。終わったら、役割を交代しましょう。

Aさん＝ [　　] 内のどちらかの語を選び、①～⑤の文全体をランダムに音読する
Bさん＝何も見ずにAさんの音読を聞き、それが true か false かを判定する。
さらに、true ならそのまま繰り返し、false なら訂正する。

① PET is the [most / second most] commonly used material for soft drink bottles in Japan.

② The content and size of PET bottles have been [unchanged / diversified] since the plastic was first used.

③ Printing is done on [labels / PET bottles themselves] to make recycling easier or possible.

④ The key to [horizontal recycling / downcycling] is the cleanliness of the collected bottles.

⑤ Soft drink manufacturers [want / do not want] recycling bins to be used as dustbins.

Oral Reading

 DL 081 CD3-30

音声イメージが可視化された文を見ながら音声を聞き、まねて音読しましょう。

太い部分は長めに、それ以外は短めに、(　) 内の音は呑み込むように、‿の部分はリンキングして、/ の部分ではポーズを置いて発音します。

1. Manufac**turing com**panies‿a**gree(d)** / tha(t) **bot**tles were to be **clear** an(d) **made sole**ly of **PET**, / with **no** di**rec(t) print**ing on them.

> POINT　that 節の that はごく軽く発音する。

2. Con**tam**ina**tion makes PE(T) bot**tle **recy**cling ex**pen**sive‿an(d) **dif**ficult‿a(t) **best** / and‿im**pos**sible‿a(t) **worst**.

> POINT　expensive and difficult と impossible の対比、best と worst の対比を意識して音読する。

3. Horizontal **recy**cling / re**sults**‿in‿a **six**ty per**cen(t)** re**duc**tion‿in **car**bon di**ox**ide / com**pare(d)** to cre**at**ing **new PET** from **fos**sil-**based re**sources.

> POINT　percent は per 部分の音色が暗く、アクセントは cent 部分にある。

Defining

1. ①〜⑧の定義に当てはまる語を本文から選んで原形を書き、音声で確認しましょう。

2. 次のペアワークをしましょう。終わったら、役割を交代しましょう。

> Aさん＝教科書を見ながらランダムに①〜⑧の定義を言う
> Bさん＝何も見ずにAさんの定義に該当する単語を答える

① (c _ _ _) = to control or limit

② (b _ _ _ _ _ _ _) = a drink, especially other than water

③ (c _ _ _ _ _ _ _ _ _ _ _ _) = the state of being made dirty, polluted, and harmful

④ (p _ _ _ _ _ _) = to help something to develop or increase

⑤ (f _ _ _ _ _) = the remains of prehistoric animals or plants preserved in rock

⑥ (m _ _ _ _ _ _ _ _ _ _ _) = a person or company that makes goods for sale

⑦ (t _ _ _ _ _ _ _ _ _ _) = allowing light to pass through it so that objects behind it can be seen

⑧ (c _ _ _ _) = a belief, aim, or principle that a group of people support or fight for

Repeating

1. ①〜⑧の空欄を**Defining**の正解の語あるいはその変化形・派生語で埋め、音声で確認しましょう。**Defining**のそれぞれの語は一度しか使えません。

2. 次のペアワークをしましょう。終わったら、役割を交代しましょう。

> Aさん＝教科書を見ながらランダムに①〜⑧を1文ずつ音読する
> Bさん＝何も見ずにそれを繰り返す
>
> Aさん＝（　　　）の箇所を「ピー」に代えて、①〜⑧の文をランダムに音読する
> Bさん＝（　　　）内の単語を答える

① The water is so (　　　　　　　　　　) that we can clearly see the bottom of the river.

② It is naturally cheaper to buy direct from the (　　　　　　　　　　).

③ Do you admire people who are willing to die for a (　　　　　　　　　　)?

④ You need to learn to (　　　　　　　　　　) your temper.

⑤ (　　　　　　　　　　) records suggest that the region was once covered by water.

⑥ A variety of (　　　　　　　　　　) are available at the snack counter.

⑦ The government should do more to (　　　　　　　　　　) renewable energy.

⑧ Landfills can (　　　　　　　　　　) drinking water if they are not properly constructed.

Retelling 🎧 DL 084 💿 CD3-33

次のキーワードを利用しながら本文の要約を言ってみましょう。例は音声で確認できます。

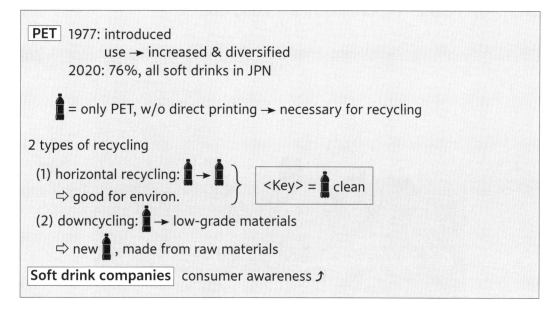

Commenting 🎧 DL 085 💿 CD3-34

1〜10は本文の内容に関連するコメントです。自分の考えに似たコメントがあれば組み合わせたり、意見を付け加えたりして、自分の考えとしてパートナーに伝えてみましょう。

1. Whenever I throw away PET bottles, I rinse them with water and remove the caps and labels.
2. When I threw away PET bottles, I took the labels off, but I never rinsed them.
3. Until now, I have always thrown away PET bottles without removing the labels.
4. From now on, I will be careful not to throw away dirty PET bottles, so that horizontal recycling is possible.
5. I carry a water bottle instead of PET bottles.
6. People need to be aware of the current low horizontal recycling rate.
7. I would like to know what the downcycled PET bottles are used for.
8. I have seen orange recycling bins.
9. It would be easier to recycle in public places if there were facilities for rinsing water and boxes for caps and labels next to the PET bottle recycling bins.
10. The PET bottle itself should have clear instructions on how to dispose of it.

Japanese Teachers Needed

日本語教師不足をボランティアで埋めるのか

Group Domenica

Reading

CD3-35 ~ CD3-43

1   Every week in community centers and other public spaces across Japan,
2 thousands of volunteers work alongside a much smaller number of professional
3 teachers to help foreign residents learn the country's language through low-cost
4 "Japanese classroom" initiatives. Receiving government support, the classrooms
5 are the only ones that many foreigners will enter to improve their Japanese skills
6 once they arrive.

7   But as Japan sees its foreign population rise again after the hit from the
8 pandemic, is it fair to rely on the goodwill of volunteers to provide a lifeline to so
9 many people new to the country?

10   Reiko Hayashikawa, representative of the Tokyo Nihongo Volunteer Network
11 and a committed volunteer for 40 years, says there are limits to what untrained
12 individuals alone can do. "Volunteers are not teachers ... What we most need is
13 for local governments to take responsibility for absolute beginners," Hayashikawa
14 said.

15   She, and others, including participants, point out that in practice, the classes
16 are often less concerned with formal language education than with offering a space

for foreigners to meet local people and discuss their concerns.

According to Immigration Services Agency of Japan data, the number of foreigners in Japan rose from some 2.76 million at the end of 2021 to around 2.96 million as of June 2022, meaning demand for language education is likely to increase. The Agency for Cultural Affairs estimates that in 2021 there were around 1,350 local Japanese classrooms operating with some 23,700 teachers, of whom about 18,750 are volunteers. There are believed to be some 300 active classrooms in Tokyo alone, which are often free or just 100 yen ($0.75) per session. Tuition for a year of full-time study at many of the capital's language schools, meanwhile, typically costs between 700,000 and 1 million yen per year.

Haruo Fukushima, a volunteer and the 94-year-old head of Group Domenica, a Japanese classroom held on Sunday afternoons in Tokyo's Adachi Ward—where around 5 percent of residents are foreign nationals—said that with many of the group's volunteers now in their 60s or older, it is struggling to find new people to meet rising demand. "We've tried recruiting even at local universities to get young people, but I think it's hard for them to ask young students to work for free."

Among the regular attendees is 36-year-old Chinese IT worker Zhang Tianwang, who described the group as "invaluable" to him. "At work, I hardly get to speak Japanese with my colleagues, so I try to come here every time."

Some students have a different opinion about nonprofessional volunteers. Katelind Ikuma, an American living in Tokyo, turned to paid lessons after attending multiple classes. "A lot of the teachers, when they found out I spoke English, wanted to practice English rather than speak Japanese," she said.

Miyako Semba, a part-time language teacher who also runs four volunteer classrooms for the international association in Hitachinaka, Ibaraki Prefecture, said the involvement of volunteers is "unavoidable" under the current pressures, but that she would prefer they did not do actual teaching work. "For me, an ideal local classroom is one where volunteers do not teach, but give people an insight into what life here is like," she said.

Kyodo

(528 words)

ℓ.18 Immigration Services Agency of Japan「出入国在留管理庁」

Chunking

 DL 086　CD3-44

1. ①～㉕の日本語に相当する表現のかたまりを本文から抜き出し、音声で確認しましょう。

（　　）内の数字は語数を表し、数字の後に「／分」とあれば、該当部分が本文中で連続していないことを表します。

2. 次のペアワークをしましょう。終わったら、役割を交代しましょう。

Ａさん＝教科書を見ながらランダムに①～㉕の日本語を言う
Ｂさん＝何も見ずにＡさんの日本語に該当する英語を答える

① 外国人の住民の日本語学習を助ける（7）	
② 政府の支援を受けており（3）	
③ 多くの外国人が入る唯一の教室（8）	
④ ボランティアの善意に頼る（6）	
⑤ 頼みの綱を提供する（3）	
⑥ 40年来の熱心なボランティア（6）	
⑦ 訓練を受けていない個人だけでできること（6）	
⑧ 自治体が責任を持つこと（6）	
⑨ 実際には（2）	
⑩ 正式の言語教育（3）	
⑪ 地域の人と会って悩みを相談する（7）	
⑫ 2021年末の（5）	
⑬ 2022年6月時点で（4）	
⑭ 言語教育に対する需要（4）	
⑮ 文化庁（5）	
⑯ 約23,700名の教員（3）	
⑰ 一回の授業につき（2）	
⑱ 年間の授業（料）（4）	
⑲ 外国籍の人たち（2）	
⑳ 新人を見つけるのに苦労している（6）	
㉑ 需要の高まりに応えるために（4）	
㉒ 若い学生にただで働いてくれるよう頼む（7）	
㉓ 同僚とは日本語を話す機会がほとんどない（8）	
㉔ 有料の授業に乗り換えた（4）	
㉕ ここでの暮らしがどのようなものかを人々に知ってもらう（10）	

Choosing

 DL 087 ● CD3-45

1. ①〜⑤の［　　］内のどちらの語を選ぶとtrueになるか考え、音声で確認しましょう。

2. 次のペアワークをしましょう。終わったら、役割を交代しましょう。

Aさん=［　　］内のどちらかの語を選び、①〜⑤の文全体をランダムに音読する
Bさん=何も見ずにAさんの音読を聞き、それがtrueかfalseかを判定する。
さらに、trueならそのまま繰り返し、falseなら訂正する。

① The "Japanese classroom" initiative aims to help [tourists / residents] whose native language is not Japanese.

② Hayashikawa's comments imply that it is particularly difficult for a volunteer to teach [beginners with zero knowledge / advanced learners].

③ It is estimated that almost [70% / 80%] of teachers in local Japanese classrooms are volunteers.

④ Semba [would / would not] like to see a division of labor between the volunteers and the professional teachers.

⑤ What seems to be needed is to [increase / decrease] public funding to hire professional Japanese teachers.

Oral Reading

 DL 088 ● CD3-46

音声イメージが可視化された文を見ながら音声を聞き、まねて音読しましょう。

太い部分は長めに、それ以外は短めに、（　）内の音は呑み込むように、‿の部分はリンキングして、/ の部分ではポーズを置いて発音します。

1. Thousands‿of **vol**un**teers work** / a**longside**‿a **much smal**ler **num**ber‿of pro**fes**sional **teach**ers / to **help for**eign **res**idents **learn Jap**anese.

> POINT　workとlearnの母音は同じで、暗い音色を持つ。

2. The **clas**ses‿are **of**ten **less** con**cerned** / with **for**mal **lan**guage‿**ed**u**ca**tion / than with‿**of**fering‿a **space** / for **for**eigners to **mee(t) lo**cal **peo**ple.

> POINT　less concerned with A than with Bという比較構文であることを意識する。

3. An‿i**deal lo**cal **classroom** / is **one** where **vol**un**teers** do **no(t) teach**, / bu(t) **give peo**ple / an‿**in**sight‿into **wha(t) life here**‿is like.

> POINT　関係副詞のwhereは弱めに発音し、前後の内容語のほうを目立たせる。

Defining

1. ①〜⑧の定義に当てはまる語を本文から選んで書き、音声で確認しましょう。

2. 次のペアワークをしましょう。終わったら、役割を交代しましょう。

> Aさん＝教科書を見ながらランダムに①〜⑧の定義を言う
> Bさん＝何も見ずにAさんの定義に該当する単語を答える

① (c _ _ _ _ _ _) = anxiety; worry

② (o _ _ _ _ _ _) = to be managed and run in a specified way

③ (s _ _ _ _ _ _) = a period of time used for a particular activity

④ (t _ _ _ _ _ _) = a sum of money charged for being taught at an educational institution

⑤ (n _ _ _ _ _ _ _) = a citizen of a particular country

⑥ (i _ _ _ _ _ _ _ _ _) = extremely useful and indispensable

⑦ (m _ _ _ _ _ _ _) = many and often varied

⑧ (i _ _ _ _ _ _) = a deep understanding

Repeating

DL 090 CD3-48

1. ①〜⑧の空欄を **Defining** の正解の語あるいはその変化形・派生語で埋め、音声で確認しましょう。**Defining** のそれぞれの語は一度しか使えません。

2. 次のペアワークをしましょう。終わったら、役割を交代しましょう。

> Aさん＝教科書を見ながらランダムに①〜⑧を1文ずつ音読する
> Bさん＝何も見ずにそれを繰り返す
> Aさん＝ (　　　) の箇所を「ピー」に代えて、①〜⑧の文をランダムに音読する
> Bさん＝ (　　　) 内の単語を答える

① We are having a brainstorming (　　　　　　　　　　) on Thursday.

② Today the internet is an (　　　　　　　　　) source of information.

③ College (　　　　　　　) in the United States is generally higher than that in Japan.

④ The machine can (　　　　　　　) for 15 hours continuously at full power.

⑤ No Japanese (　　　　　　　) are reported to have been involved in the accident.

⑥ Studying in Australia for a year gave me a valuable (　　　　　　　　) into Aboriginal culture.

⑦ This poison is known to cause (　　　　　　　　　) organ failure.

⑧ There is general agreement that global warming is one of the greatest (　　　　　　　) of our time.

Retelling

DL 091 CD3-49

次のキーワードを利用しながら本文の要約を言ってみましょう。例は音声で確認できます。

Foreigners → JPN
number ♪
Many w/o sufficient knowledge of Japanese
⇨ demand for Japanese lang. classes ♪

Ideally: students ←teach— qualified, professional teachers
Reality: qualified, professional teachers < volunteers
↑
lack professional skills to teach lang.
⇨ classroom = place, foreigners, meet locals
discuss concerns

One teacher "actual teaching ← by professional teachers, not volunteers"
↑
public funding needed

Commenting

DL 092 CD3-50

1〜10は本文の内容に関連するコメントです。自分の考えに似たコメントがあれば組み合わせたり、意見を付け加えたりして、自分の考えとしてパートナーに伝えてみましょう。

1. I would like to become a Japanese teacher.

2. Volunteers should be responsible for things other than teaching Japanese.

3. The government should provide more financial support for Japanese language teaching.

4. I was surprised by the huge price difference between volunteer-assisted classes and commercial language schools.

5. We should establish a public system for teaching Japanese to those who come to live in Japan.

6. I would like to help foreigners as a Japanese volunteer.

7. If it is possible to volunteer online, I would like to help.

8. We could improve the situation of Japanese language teaching in cooperation with private companies that want to attract foreign personnel.

9. If there is a system where foreigners and Japanese can learn each other's native language, the number of volunteers may increase.

10. In addition to Japanese language classes, more opportunities should be created for foreigners living in Japan to get together.

The Backyard Ultra Marathon: It is easy ... until it is not

なぜ 3 日も 4 日も走り続けるマラソンなのか

Daiki Shibawaki

Reading

CD3-51 ~ CD3-60

1   The rules are simple: Runners start on the hour. When they complete their
2 6.71-kilometer "yard," the rest of the hour is spent eating, sleeping and preparing
3 in whatever other ways they see fit until the start of the next hour when they must
4 do it again. Run quickly and you have more time for recovery but risk burning out
5 early; run slowly and you conserve energy but sacrifice recovery time.

6   It's a straightforward contest with one major catch: No one knows how many
7 yards runners will have to complete to win, and hundreds of athletes are trying
8 to outlast each other across the globe all at the same time. It is less a race than a
9 last-person standing endurance test—less an ultramarathon than a battle of wills.

10   It's the Backyard Ultra, and last October, several Japanese runners found out
11 just how grueling it can be. Tomokazu Ihara, a renowned Japanese ultrarunner,
12 was the director of Team Japan's satellite race for this year's Backyard Ultra World
13 Championship.

14   The event's original conception comes from the mind of Lazarus "Laz" Lake
15 (an American runner). Lake held the first Backyard Ultra on his own property in
16 Morgan County, Tennessee, in 2012, but the event has since ballooned into 402

officially recognized events held across the globe. The 15 top-performing Japanese 17 runners were invited to the October 15 satellite tournament overseen by Ihara. 18

Thirty-seven countries participated in the tournament, which officially began 19 at 7 a.m. Central Standard Time (Lake's home time zone). For runners in Japan, 20 that meant preparing themselves for athletic exertions of indeterminate length 21 from 10 p.m. Luckily, Japan was blessed with good weather; other teams faced a 22 typhoon, a blizzard and a wildfire. 23

According to Ihara, the first 24 hours are "just a warmup." Indeed, every 24 Japanese runner completed their first 24 yards without much trouble. After that, 25 however, runners began throwing in the towel. After 48 hours and more than 320 26 kilometers, only seven Japanese runners carried on. Well into the third full day of 27 competition, only four Japanese runners remained. 28

Eventually, Daiki Shibawaki was "the last samurai standing," as Ihara likes 29 to say—but even though he'd already been running for more than three days 30 straight, Shibawaki had one more yard to complete before claiming victory among 31 the Japanese competitors. Just before 12 p.m. on October 19 and after running 32 over 576 kilometers, Shibawaki returned to the goal for the last time. 33

"Earlier in the race when my mind was clearer, it felt more difficult because I 34 was thinking about the long road ahead," Shibawaki says. "As more people dropped 35 out, it became easier because that meant that the finish was getting closer and I 36 could finally rest and take a bath." 37

Ultimately, it was just two runners from Belgium who outlasted Shibawaki 38 and set a new world record by completing 101 yards each. When they both decided 39 to retire together, Lake decreed that Belgium would have no official winner—just 40 two "assists" for second-place finishers. 41

Like Shibawaki, however, the Belgian co-winners are assured a spot in 42 next October's global final championship at Lake's home in Tennessee. Like all 43 participants, they also received medals bearing Lake's personal slogan: "It is easy 44 … until it is not." 45

The Japan Times

(536 words)

 Notes

ℓ.16 balloon「（風船のように）ふくらむ」   ℓ.20 Central Standard Time「（米国の）中部標準時」

ℓ.27 carry on「（諦めずに）続ける」   ℓ.41 assist「アシスト（スポーツで得点を助けるプレー）」

ℓ.44 bear「（印などを）有する」

Chunking

DL 093 　 CD3-61

1. ①～㉕の日本語に相当する表現のかたまりを本文から抜き出し、音声で確認しましょう。
（　）内の数字は語数を表し、数字の後に「／分」とあれば、該当部分が本文中で連続していないことを表します。

2. 次のペアワークをしましょう。終わったら、役割を交代しましょう。

　　Aさん＝教科書を見ながらランダムに①～㉕の日本語を言う
　　Bさん＝何も見ずにAさんの日本語に該当する英語を答える

---

① 正時に（〜時00分という瞬間に）（3）
② その他何でも、自分が良いと思うやり方で（7）
③ 早く体力がなくなる危険を冒す（4）
④ 回復時間を犠牲にする（3）
⑤ 勝つには何「ヤード」走らねばならぬのか（10）
⑥ 他人が脱落した後まで走る（3）
⑦ 全世界で同時に（8）
⑧ ウルトラマラソンというより意志の闘い（8）
⑨ いかに過酷なものになり得るか（5）
⑩ 元々の着想（2）
⑪ 彼個人の土地で（4）
⑫ 長さが決まっていない激しい運動（5）
⑬ 良い天候に恵まれた（5）
⑭ ギブアップしはじめた（5）
⑮ 競技3日目のかなり経った時点で（8）
⑯ 3日を超えてずっと走っている（8）
⑰ あと1「ヤード」走らねばならなかった（6）
⑱ 国内優勝の称号を勝ち取る前に（7）
⑲ 最後のゴールインをした（8）
⑳ 精神的によりきつかった（4）
㉑ 先の長い道のりを思って（6）
㉒ ついに休んで風呂に入る（6）
㉓ 新たな世界記録を打ち立てる（5）
㉔ 一緒に離脱すると決めた（4）
㉕ 出場枠を保証される（4）

Choosing

 DL 094 CD3-62

1. ①〜⑤の [   ] 内のどちらの語を選ぶと true になるか考え、音声で確認しましょう。

2. 次のペアワークをしましょう。終わったら、役割を交代しましょう。

> Aさん＝ [   ] 内のどちらかの語を選び、①〜⑤の文全体をランダムに音読する
> Bさん＝何も見ずにAさんの音読を聞き、それがtrueかfalseかを判定する。
> さらに、trueならそのまま繰り返し、falseなら訂正する。

① This race is about how [long / fast] you can keep running, with or without hourly rests.

② It is assumed that competitors can run 6.71 kilometers in under [30 / 60] minutes.

③ As long as you [can restart on the hour / do not fall asleep], it does not matter how you spend your rest time.

④ The race is not over as long as there [is at least one runner / are at least three runners] still running.

⑤ To win the satellite race in your country, you [have / don't have] to be the only runner left in your country.

Oral Reading

 DL 095 CD3-63

音声イメージが可視化された文を見ながら音声を聞き、まねて音読しましょう。

太い部分は長めに、それ以外は短めに、(   ) 内の音は呑み込むように、‿の部分はリンキングして、/ の部分ではポーズを置いて発音します。

1. Run quickly / and‿you **have more time** for re**cov**ery / bu(t) **risk burn**ing‿**out ear**ly; / **run slow**ly / and‿you con**serve‿en**ergy / but **sac**ri**fice** re**cov**ery **time**.

> POINT run と risk の語頭のR音、quickly と slowly の語中のL音を確実に出す。

2. No one **knows how man**y **yards** / **run**ners will **have** to com**ple(te)** to **win**.

> POINT no も knows も母音は二重母音。

3. As **more peo**ple **dro(pp)ed‿out**, / i(t) be**came‿eas**ier / be**cause tha(t) mean(t)** tha(t) the **fin**ish was **get**ting **clos**er / and‿I could **fi**nally **rest‿**an(d) **take‿**a **bath**.

> POINT dropped では pp の音は聞こえず、ed にあたる t 音が次の out とリンキングする。

Defining

1. ①〜⑧の定義に当てはまる語を本文から選んで書き、音声で確認しましょう。

2. 次のペアワークをしましょう。終わったら、役割を交代しましょう。

> Aさん＝教科書を見ながらランダムに①〜⑧の定義を言う
> Bさん＝何も見ずにAさんの定義に該当する単語を答える

① (c _ _ _ _ _ _ _) = to avoid the wasteful overuse of

② (s _ _ _ _ _ _ _ _) = to give up, for the sake of something else

③ (o _ _ _ _ _ _) = to continue to exist for a longer time than something else

④ (e _ _ _ _ _ _ _ _) = the ability to continue doing something difficult or painful for a long time

⑤ (r _ _ _ _ _ _ _) = known or talked about by many people

⑥ (c _ _ _ _ _ _ _ _ _) = the forming of a plan or idea

⑦ (p _ _ _ _ _ _ _) = a building and the land belonging to it

⑧ (e _ _ _ _ _ _ _) = physical or mental effort

Repeating

1. ①〜⑧の空欄を **Defining** の正解の語あるいはその変化形・派生語で埋め、音声で確認しましょう。**Defining** のそれぞれの語は一度しか使えません。

2. 次のペアワークをしましょう。終わったら、役割を交代しましょう。

> Aさん＝教科書を見ながらランダムに①〜⑧を1文ずつ音読する
> Bさん＝何も見ずにそれを繰り返す
> Aさん＝（　　　）の箇所を「ピー」に代えて、①〜⑧の文をランダムに音読する
> Bさん＝（　　　）内の単語を答える

① Running on a regular basis improves strength and (　　　　　　　　).

② (　　　　　　　　　　) is generally less expensive in rural areas than it is in urban areas.

③ It is ridiculous to (　　　　　　　　) your personal life for your work.

④ It is he that (　　　　　　　　) the idea of turning the old school into a giant café.

⑤ A leather sofa will usually (　　　　　　　　) a fabric sofa, so it is worth the price.

⑥ One week before the marathon, avoid any physical (　　　　　　　　).

⑦ Everyone needs to make efforts to (　　　　　　　　) water.

⑧ She is (　　　　　　　　) for her advocacy of human rights.

Retelling

 DL 098   CD3-66

次のキーワードを利用しながら本文の要約を言ってみましょう。例は音声で確認できます。

Backyard Ultra | grueling endurance

Rule: start on the hour (e.g., 5:00, 6:00, 7:00, ... 13:00, 14:00, ...)

run a "yard" (= 6.71 km), <u>any speed</u>

run fast ⟶ tired early, more time to recover

run slowly → conserve energy, less time to recover

No one knows, how many yards, cover to win

⇨ race goes on, someone keeps going

Recent Backyard Ultra

Japanese winner: 576 km, more than 3 days

a new world record, 2 Belgians: 101 yards = 678 km

Commenting

 DL 099   CD3-67

1～10は本文の内容に関連するコメントです。自分の考えに似たコメントがあれば組み合わせたり、意見を付け加えたりして、自分の考えとしてパートナーに伝えてみましょう。

1. I just hate running.

2. I am an athlete, but this race is not for me.

3. It is definitely not good for the human body to keep running like this.

4. I want to run an ultramarathon (e.g., a 100 km marathon) one day.

5. I want to experience what it feels like to run for three days straight.

6. I am a fan of Haruki Murakami and he is a runner, so I feel close to this race.

7. I don't understand why anyone would want to run such a grueling race.

8. The slogan "it is easy ... until it is not" appealed to me.

9. It would be fairer if all participants ran at the same place.

10. I think it is crazy but romantic that all the competitors around the world are running at the same time at their own places, no matter what the local conditions are.

Beware of Your Digital Footprint

その書き込み、誰に見られても OK ですか

Reading

⊙ CD3-68 ～ ⊙ CD3-79

1　　　Aly Drake says she used TikTok like a diary. When she felt friendless, she'd
2　make a video about it. When she noticed the symptoms of her bipolar disorder
3　she'd open the app and press record. On TikTok, her videos reached people who
4　understood her and what she was going through, she said.

5　　　But her videos also reached the coaches of the college water ski program she
6　hoped to join. They sent her an email saying her videos were "too negative," she
7　said. And she was denied a spot on the team. "I was just talking about how I feel.
8　It's supposed to be a good thing to do that," Drake, who has 4,000 TikTok followers,
9　said. Drake ended up starting her college application process from scratch.

10　　　Drake and her peers are in a tough spot. Raised on the internet and isolated
11　by the pandemic, their social lives have played out on apps like TikTok. But as
12　they encounter college or the working world, they're met with a harsh reality:
13　What older generations think is respectable hasn't changed.

14　　　College preparatory companies urge students to mind their "digital footprints,"
15　or the trail they leave when posting or commenting online, during the application
16　process, said Robert Franek, editor in chief of the Princeton Review. After all, he

said, an authentic social media profile can give an applicant an advantage. 17

But it could also ruin an applicant's chances. Sometimes, the app's design leads 18 young people to make videos hiring managers or admissions officers won't like, said 19 Stephanie Rowe, a 19-year-old applied computer science student and TikTok user. 20

When Rowe saw what appeared to be underage girls posting videos of 21 themselves wearing underwear in response to a trending sound, she made a video 22 urging other users to think of their digital footprints. 23

It blew up, receiving more than 19 million views. The response was mixed, Rowe 24 said. Some people agreed on the importance (and scariness) of digital footprints. 25 Others accused her of slut-shaming, and that criticism hurt, she said. 26

Reviewing candidates' social media profiles can open the door for discrimination, 27 said Michael Zimmer, director of the Center for Data, Ethics, and Society at 28 Marquette University. What's considered offensive for a teen girl to post, for 29 instance, may look like harmless fun if a teen boy posts it. 30

But social media checks also help prevent discrimination on campus— 31 Marquette withdrew a student's admission offer in 2020 because of a racist social 32 media post about the murder of George Floyd. 33

Even on public platforms, a user's intended audience is often peers, not 34 suit-and-tie wearing recruiters. It's up to employers and admissions professionals 35 to understand the context in which something was posted, Zimmer said. That 36 takes empathy and cultural understanding, so the greater risk is that universities 37 and employers hand off the responsibility to AI that scans applicants' accounts for 38 red flags, he noted. 39

Instead of portraying themselves as perfect and pleasant on social media, 40 students should make their profiles consistent with the materials they submit to 41 universities, Zimmer said. In other words: If you wrote an essay vowing to end 42 cruelty to animals, don't post that video where you startle a sleeping cow. 43

Drake, for her part, has stopped making TikToks when she feels lonely or 44 depressed. She avoids alcohol and curse words in her posts and tries to keep her 45 digital footprint in mind, she said. 46

The Washington Post

(560 words)

 Notes

ℓ.10 a tough spot「難しい状況［立場］」 ℓ.11 play out「起こる、展開する」

ℓ.26 slut-shaming「スラット・シェイミング（古い女性観に基づく偏見から、女性の外見や行動を非難して貶めること。slut は『性的にだらしのない女』という意味の卑語。）」

ℓ.43 startle「びっくりさせる」

Chunking

 DL 100　 CD3-80

1. ①〜㉕の日本語に相当する表現のかたまりを本文から抜き出し、音声で確認しましょう。

（　）内の数字は語数を表し、数字の後に「／分」とあれば、該当部分が本文中で連続していないことを表します。

2. 次のペアワークをしましょう。終わったら、役割を交代しましょう。

　Aさん＝教科書を見ながらランダムに①〜㉕の日本語を言う
　Bさん＝何も見ずにAさんの日本語に該当する英語を答える

① 自分の双極性障害の症状（6）	
② 彼女が経験していることを理解した（6／分）	
③ 入部を断られた（7）	
④ 大学受験をゼロから始めること（7）	
⑤ ネットで育ち感染爆発で孤立し（9）	
⑥ 大学や実社会に出会う（6）	
⑦ 上の世代がまともだと思う事柄（6）	
⑧ 自分が残す足跡を気にするよう学生に呼びかける（8／分）	
⑨ オンラインで投稿したり書き込んだりする時（5）	
⑩ 志願者に有利に働く（5）	
⑪ 採用担当者や入試選考担当者（5）	
⑫ 下着姿の自撮り動画を投稿している（6）	
⑬ 差別を招き入れる可能性がある（6）	
⑭ 10代の少女が投稿するのは不快と思われること（9）	
⑮ 大学内での差別を防ぐ助けになる（5）	
⑯ ある学生の入学内定を取り消した（5）	
⑰ 人種差別的なSNSの投稿（5）	
⑱ 意図された視聴者層（2）	
⑲ 共感と文化的理解が必要だ（5）	
⑳ その責任をAIに委ねる（6）	
㉑ 危険な兆候がないか応募者のアカウントをスキャンする（6）	
㉒ 完璧で好感のもてる自分を描き出すこと（6）	
㉓ 大学に提出する資料（6）	
㉔ 動物虐待を終わりにすると誓うエッセイ（8）	
㉕ 飲酒と罵り言葉を避ける（5）	

Choosing 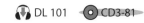 DL 101 CD3-81

1. ①〜⑤の [   ] 内のどちらの語を選ぶと true になるか考え、音声で確認しましょう。
2. 次のペアワークをしましょう。終わったら、役割を交代しましょう。

Aさん＝ [   ] 内のどちらかの語を選び、①〜⑤の文全体をランダムに音読する
Bさん＝何も見ずにAさんの音読を聞き、それがtrueかfalseかを判定する。
さらに、trueならそのまま繰り返し、falseなら訂正する。

① Drake was quite honest about herself on TikTok, which [positively / negatively] affected the coaches' assessment of her.

② It is implied that the younger generation uses social media [more / less] because of the recent pandemic.

③ Franek [is / is not] suggesting that students applying to universities should avoid posting or commenting online.

④ Rowe posted a video [because / not because] she wanted people to be aware of their digital footprint.

⑤ The article suggests that checking candidates' social media [can / can't] work both ways in terms of discrimination.

Oral Reading  DL 102 CD3-82

音声イメージが可視化された文を見ながら音声を聞き、まねて音読しましょう。
太い部分は長めに、それ以外は短めに、（　）内の音は呑み込むように、‿の部分はリンキングして、/ の部分ではポーズを置いて発音します。

1. College pre**parato**ry **com**panies **urge stu**dents to **min(d)** their "**dig**ital **footprints**," / or the **trail** they **leave** / when **post**ing‿or **com**menting‿**online**.

POINT digitalのgi部分は、「ジ」でなく「ヂ」/dʒɪ/（破擦音）である。

2. Review**ing can**di**dates' so**cial **me**dia **pro**files / can‿**o**pen the **door** for dis**crimina**tion, / but‿i(t) can‿**al**so **hel(p)** pre**ven(t)** dis**crimina**tion‿on **cam**pus.

POINT canのあとに母音で始まる語が来たら、必ずnでリンキングさせる。

3. Instead‿of por**tray**ing them**selves**‿as **per**fe(c)t‿and **pleas**ant‿on **so**cial **me**dia, / **stu**dents should **ma(ke)** their **pro**files con**sis**ten(t) with the ma**te**rials they su(b)**mi(t)** to **uni**ver**sities.

POINT mediaをカタカナ的に「メディア」と言わない。

Defining

 DL 103　CD3-83

1. ①〜⑧の定義に当てはまる語を本文から選んで書き、音声で確認しましょう。

2. 次のペアワークをしましょう。終わったら、役割を交代しましょう。

Aさん＝教科書を見ながらランダムに①〜⑧の定義を言う
Bさん＝何も見ずにAさんの定義に該当する単語を答える

① (s _ _ _ _ _ _) = a physical or mental feature which is regarded as indicating a condition of disease

② (a _ _ _ _ _ _ _ _ _ _) = a formal request to an authority for something

③ (p _ _ _) = a person of the same age or status as another person

④ (r _ _ _ _ _ _ _ _ _) = regarded by society to be good, proper, and decent

⑤ (c _ _ _ _ _ _ _ _) = a person who is being considered for a job or position

⑥ (o _ _ _ _ _ _ _ _) = causing someone to be upset or angry because it is rude or insulting

⑦ (p _ _ _ _ _ _) = to describe or represent in a particular way

⑧ (s _ _ _ _ _) = to present (something) to someone in authority for consideration

Repeating

 DL 104　CD3-84

1. ①〜⑧の空欄を **Defining** の正解の語あるいはその変化形・派生語で埋め、音声で確認しましょう。**Defining** のそれぞれの語は一度しか使えません。

2. 次のペアワークをしましょう。終わったら、役割を交代しましょう。

Aさん＝教科書を見ながらランダムに①〜⑧を1文ずつ音読する
Bさん＝何も見ずにそれを繰り返す

Aさん＝（　　）の箇所を「ピー」に代えて、①〜⑧の文をランダムに音読する
Bさん＝（　　）内の単語を答える

① I hope you can all (　　　　　　　　　　　) your reports before the deadline.

② In the upcoming election, 60 (　　　　　　　　　　) are competing for 40 seats.

③ In this book, she is (　　　　　　　　　) as an ambitious and independent woman.

④ Teenagers may find it difficult to resist (　　　　　　　　　　) pressure.

⑤ That politician is known for making (　　　　　　　　) comments about women.

⑥ The first (　　　　　　　　　) of the disease is a very high fever.

⑦ Put a tie on; it'll make you look more (　　　　　　　　　).

⑧ I need to know more about the job before I decide whether to (　　　　　　　　　) for it.

Retelling

 DL 105　CD3-85

次のキーワードを利用しながら本文の要約を言ってみましょう。例は音声で確認できます。

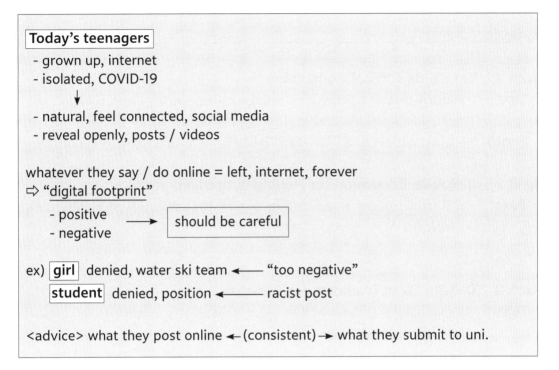

Today's teenagers
- grown up, internet
- isolated, COVID-19
　↓
- natural, feel connected, social media
- reveal openly, posts / videos

whatever they say / do online = left, internet, forever
⇨ "digital footprint"
- positive ——→ should be careful
- negative

ex) girl denied, water ski team ◄—— "too negative"
　　student denied, position ◄——— racist post

<advice> what they post online ◄— (consistent) —► what they submit to uni.

Commenting

 DL 106　CD3-86

1～10は本文の内容に関連するコメントです。自分の考えに似たコメントがあれば組み合わせたり、意見を付け加えたりして、自分の考えとしてパートナーに伝えてみましょう。

1. Social media is a necessary place for me to express myself.

2. I post on social media to give myself an edge in my job search.

3. After reading this article, I have decided to stop exaggerating myself online.

4. Browsing other people's posts sometimes makes me jealous.

5. I make it a rule to only post positive things online.

6. I only post things that would not cause a problem no matter who saw them.

7. I will be careful about the digital footprint I leave behind.

8. It is not right for recruiters to see a candidate's social media posts as part of the selection process as they are the candidate's privacy.

9. I would not mind if recruiters from the company looked at my posts as these posts can help them understand me better.

10. The older generation should update their views on social media.

Acknowledgements

All the materials are reprinted by permission of the copyright holders.

Credits

Unit 1   Let Us Be Ethical Consumers
Text   Apparel makers tapping into ethical consumption
JIJI / The Japan News, May 31, 2022 (partially modified)
Photo   EQUALAND -TRUST AND INTIMATE- / Produced by ONEO Ltd.

Unit 2   Inclusive Education for People With Disabilities
Text   U.N. panel urges Japan to end segregated education of children with disabilities
Kyodo / The Japan Times, September 10, 2022 (partially modified)

Unit 3   Debate Over Transgender Athletes
Text   Transgender athletes weigh in on debate over participation in sports following FINA decision
ABC (Australian Broadcasting Corporation), July 14, 2022 (partially modified)

Unit 4   Robots as Family Members to Love
Text   Japan's emotionally enhanced robots—and the people who love them
The Japan Times, November 13, 2022 (partially modified)
Photo   GROOVE X

Unit 5   Japan's Baby Stroller War
Text   Japan's Perennial Baby Stroller War
Unseen Japan, May 23, 2019 (partially modified)
Photo   Jiji Press Photo

Unit 6   Pay Taxes and Save Cats and People
Text   Gifu project to rescue cats using tax donation system draws backers
JIJI / The Japan Times, August 11, 2022 (partially modified)
Photo   Neco Republic

Unit 7   Easier Access to Paternity Leave
Text   Law amendment aims to make paternity leave more accessible in Japan
Kyodo / The Japan Times, April 4, 2022 (partially modified)
Photo   Jiji Press Photo

Unit 8 Veganism on the Rise
Text   Veganism on the rise among health-conscious in Japan
        Kyodo / The Japan Times, November 29, 2022 (partially modified)
Photo   Chikaranomoto Holdings Co., Ltd.

Unit 9 Same-Sex Partnership Oath System
Text   Tokyo begins recognition of same-sex partnerships
        The Japan Times, November 1, 2022 (partially modified)

Unit 10 Get Out of Japan to Earn More Money?!
Text   Concerned about the future, will more Japanese youth seek opportunities overseas?
        The Japan Times, November 27, 2022 (partially modified)

Unit 11 Baby Names Getting More Creative
Text   Across Japan, baby names are getting more creative
        The Japan Times, January 7, 2023 (partially modified)
Photo   Jiji Press Photo

Unit 12 Japanese Love Affair With PET Bottles
Text   Plastic love: Proliferation of PET bottles in Japan complicates a sustainable future
        The Japan Times, March 14, 2022 (partially modified)

Unit 13 Japanese Teachers Needed
Text   FOCUS: Volunteers taking outsized role in Japanese language support
        Kyodo, January 6, 2023 (partially modified)
Photo   Group Domenica

Unit 14 The Backyard Ultra Marathon: It is easy ... until it is not
Text   The unending agony of Japan's Backyard Ultra marathon
        The Japan Times, December 24, 2022 (partially modified)
Photo   Daiki Shibawaki

Unit 15 Beware of Your Digital Footprint
Text   TikTok loves Gen Z's true confessions. Colleges and employers, not so much.
        From The Washington Post. ©2023 The Washington Post. All rights reserved. Used under license. (partially modified)

本書にはCD（別売）があります

Reading in More Action

発信型英語リーディング

2024年1月20日　初版第1刷発行
2024年2月20日　初版第2刷発行

編著者　　　靜　　哲　人

発行者　　　福　岡　正　人

発行所　　株式会社　金星堂

（〒101-0051）　東京都千代田区神田神保町 3-21
Tel　（03）3263-3828（営業部）
（03）3263-3997（編集部）
Fax　（03）3263-0716
https://www.kinsei-do.co.jp

編集担当　池田恭子・長島吉成　　　　　　　　Printed in Japan
印刷所／日新印刷株式会社　製本所／松島製本
本書の無断複製・複写は著作権法上での例外を除き禁じられています。本書を代
行業者等の第三者に依頼してスキャンやデジタル化することは、たとえ個人や家
庭内での利用であっても認められておりません。
落丁・乱丁本はお取り替えいたします。

ISBN978-4-7647-4197-3　　C1082